English
At Your Command!

HAMPTON-BROWN

Hampton – Brown
P.O. Box 223220
Carmel, California 93922
800-333-3510
www.hampton-brown.com

Printed in the United States of America

ISBN 0-7362-1646-4   Softcover
ISBN 0-7362-1645-6   Hardcover

05 06 07 08 09 10 11 12 9 8 7 6 5 4

Hampton-Brown extends special thanks to the following consultants who contributed to the development of *English At Your Command!*

Sue Goldstein
Bilingual Team Leader / Grade 3 Teacher
Puentes Two-Way Bilingual Program
Regional Multicultural Magnet School
New London, Connecticut

Raul C. Ramirez, Jr.
Grade 3 Bilingual / Gifted and Talented Teacher
Royalgate Elementary School
South San Antonio ISD
San Antonio, Texas

Lizabeth Lepovitz
Bilingual Teacher, Grades 2, 3
J. L. Carson Elementary School
Northside ISD
San Antonio, Texas

Ruth Woods
ESL Teacher, Grades 2, 3, 4, 5
Minneapolis Public Schools
Minneapolis, Minnesota

Acknowledgments

Every effort has been made to secure permission, but if any omissions have been made, please let us know. We gratefully acknowledge permission to reprint the following material:

ZB Font Method Copyright © 1996 Zaner-Bloser.

P3, p13 and p295: "Getting About – Flyers" from *Bugs* by Gerald Legg. Copyright © 1998 Quadrillion Publishing, Ltd. Used by permission of Chrysalis Books, Ltd., London.

P103 and p219: *Two of Everything* by Lily Toy Hong. Copyright © 1993 by Lily Toy Hong. Reprinted by permission of Albert Whitman Company. All rights reserved.

P123: *Dear Juno* cover from *Dear Juno* by Soyung Pak, illustrated by Susan Kathleen Hartung. Copyright © 1999 by Susan Kathleen Hartung, illustrations. Used by permission of Viking Penguin, an imprint of Penguin Putnam Books for Young Readers, a division of Penguin Putnam, Inc. All rights reserved.

Pp144 –145: Elements of the play *Annie*, by Thomas Meehan. Used by permission of the author.

P146: "Rainy Day" by William Wise from *All On a Summer Day* published by Pantheon. Copyright © 1971 by William Wise. Reprinted by permission of Curtis Brown, Ltd.

P147: "Tommy" by Gwendolyn Brooks from *Bronzeville Boys and Girls.* Copyright © 1956 by Gwendolyn Brooks Blakely. Used by permission of HarperCollins Publishers.

P148: "There Was a Young Lady " from *The Complete Nonsense of Edward Lear.* Copyright © 1951, Dover Publications, Inc. Used by permission of the publisher.

P149: "Ears Hear" by Hymes Jr., James and Lucia, from *Oodles of Noodles.* Copyright © 1964. Reprinted by permission of Pearson Education, Inc.

P182 and p188: From TOO MANY TAMALES by Gary Soto. Illustrated by Ed Martinez, copyright © 1993 by Gary Soto, text, copyright © 1993 by Ed Martinez, illustrations. Used by permission of G.P. Putnam's Sons, a division of Penguin Young Readers Group, a member of Penguin Group (USA) Inc., 345 Hudson St., New York, NY 10014. All rights reserved.

P183: From LON PO PO by Ed Young. Copyright © 1989 by Ed Young. Used by permission of Philomel Books, a division of Penguin Young Readers Group (USA) Inc., 345 Hudson St., New York, NY 10014. All rights reserved.

P231: Facsimile page from Primary Dictionary. Copyright © 1991 Macmillan/McGraw-Hill Publishing Company. Used by permission of The McGraw-Hill Companies.

P281: "Ice Skating" by Sandra Liatsos. Copyright © 1982 by Sandra Liatsos. Used by permission of Marian Reiner.

Pp297-298 and pp300-301: *The Honey Makers* copyright © 1997 by Gail Gibbons. Used by permission of HarperCollins Publishers.

Pp297-298: Cover art from *The Life and Times of the Honeybee.* Copyright © 1995 by Charles Micucci. Used by permission of Houghton Mifflin Company. All rights reserved.

P297 and p299: Larry West, *Ranger Rick* August 1996 cover (bee). From *Ranger Rick,* used by permission of photographer.

P299: Reprinted with the permission of Simon & Schuster Books for Young Readers, an imprint of Simon & Schuster Children's Publishing Division from *Macmillan Dictionary for Children,* revised by Robert B. Costello, Editor in Chief. Copyright © 1997 Simon & Schuster.

P299 and p316: From *The World Book Encyclopedia.* Copyright © 1998 World Book, Inc. By permission of the publisher. www.worldbook.com

P317: Facsimile page from *The World Book Student Discovery Encyclopedia.* Copyright © 2002 World Book, Inc. By permission of the publisher.

P319: Tom Leeson, *Ranger Rick* January 2002 cover (coyote). From *Ranger Rick,* used by permission of the photographer.

Photography:

P32 and p33: Courtesy of the Aceves family (grandparents).

P144: Courtesy of the Fredericksburg Theatre Company, Mary Washington College, Dept. of Theatre and Dance, Fredericksburg, VA (Annie).

Animals Animals/Earth Scenes: p75 (slow turtle, © Robert Winslow), p131 (bird © Ron Willocks; fox, © Robert Maier).

Acknowledgments continued on pages 351-352.

Welcome!

In this book, you will find all kinds of ways to **communicate**. When you communicate, you say what you are thinking, feeling, and imagining. This book will help you find the words you need. It will show you how English works. You will learn how to organize your ideas and write about them. You will even learn how to do research in the library and on the Internet, too!

Whenever you have a question about English, you can look here first. This book will put **English At Your Command!**

Table of Contents

Chapter 2
Picture It!

Graphs

Story Maps

Chapter 3
Put It in Writing!

Chapter 4
Present It!

Handwriting and Spelling Guide

Chapter 5
Grammar Made Graphic

Marcus

puts it together.

Chapter 6
Look It Up!

Chapter 1
Just the Right Word

Where do you live?
What is the weather like?
What do you like to do?

You can tell about anything
with just the right word.

Words About You

My name is **Kenji**.
My address is **23 Cancha Road, San Antonio, Texas**.
My phone number is **555-6878**.

Actions

I can **read**.

I can **eat**.

I can **paint**.

I can **run**.
What can you do?

I can **write**.

I can **carry**.

Feelings

I am **confused**.

I am **sad**.

I am **surprised**.

I am **angry**.

I am **bored**.

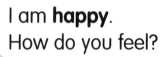

I am **happy**.
How do you feel?

Colors

 white

 purple

 brown

 yellow

 red

 pink

 orange

 gold

 green

 blue

 black

 gray

Just the Right Word

Shapes

circle

oval

square

rectangle

triangle

star

I have a **red circle**. What do you have?

Sizes

I have a **big** sandwich. What do you have?

short hair

big sandwich

little sandwich

short boy

long hair

small drink

large drink

medium drink

tall girl

Just the Right Word

Sounds

quiet whisper

noisy drum

I hear a **loud** horn. What do you hear?

Smells

sweet flower

clean towel

rotten garbage

fresh bread

I smell a **stinky** sock. What do you smell?

Touch

smooth skin

soft pillow

wet hair

hot drink

I feel a **bumpy** pineapple. What do you feel?

Tastes

sweet cake

spicy salsa

salty pretzel

tangy orange

I taste a **sour** lemon.

fresh vegetables

juicy peach

What do you taste?

tasty treat

delicious food

At Home

window

gate

apartment building

mobile home

town house

At Home

chimney

There is a **kitchen**.
There is a **living room**.
There is a **bedroom**.

curtain

counter

stove

refrigerator

cabinet

oven

kitchen

closet

nightstand

bed

dresser

bedroom

lamp

chair

couch

shower

bathtub

sink

toilet

table

living room

bathroom

Family

my father

my grandpa

my grandma

Me!

my aunt

my uncle

my cousins

Words About Your School

34

bars

playground

slide

Inside the School

Just the Right Word

library

office

girls' bathroom

cafeteria

People at School

The **teacher** teaches a student.

The **students** write.

The **librarian** finds books.

The **nurse** helps sick and hurt people.

The **custodian** cleans the school.

The **principal** leads the school.

Who works in your school?

In a Classroom

Just the Right Word

pencil

crayon

chalk

ruler

scissors

eraser

glue

This is my **classroom**.
Here is a **teacher**.
Here are some **students**.

student

Things to Do

Circle the correct picture.

Line up.

Put an X on the square.

Stand up.

Sit down.

Numbers

1 one

2 two

3 three

4 four

5 five

6 six

7 seven

8 eight

9 nine

10 ten

I have **five** buttons in each group.

More than 10

11 eleven	21 twenty-one	40 forty
12 twelve	22 twenty-two	50 fifty
13 thirteen	23 twenty-three	60 sixty
14 fourteen	24 twenty-four	70 seventy
15 fifteen	25 twenty-five	80 eighty
16 sixteen	26 twenty-six	90 ninety
17 seventeen	27 twenty-seven	100 one hundred
18 eighteen	28 twenty-eight	1,000 one thousand
19 nineteen	29 twenty-nine	
20 twenty	30 thirty	

Money

1¢ one cent

5¢ five cents

10¢ ten cents

25¢ twenty-five cents

$1 one dollar

$5 five dollars

$10 ten dollars

$20 twenty dollars

Numbers

I have **a couple of** buttons.

a few buttons

some buttons
several buttons

a lot of buttons
many buttons

Too many buttons!

Number Order

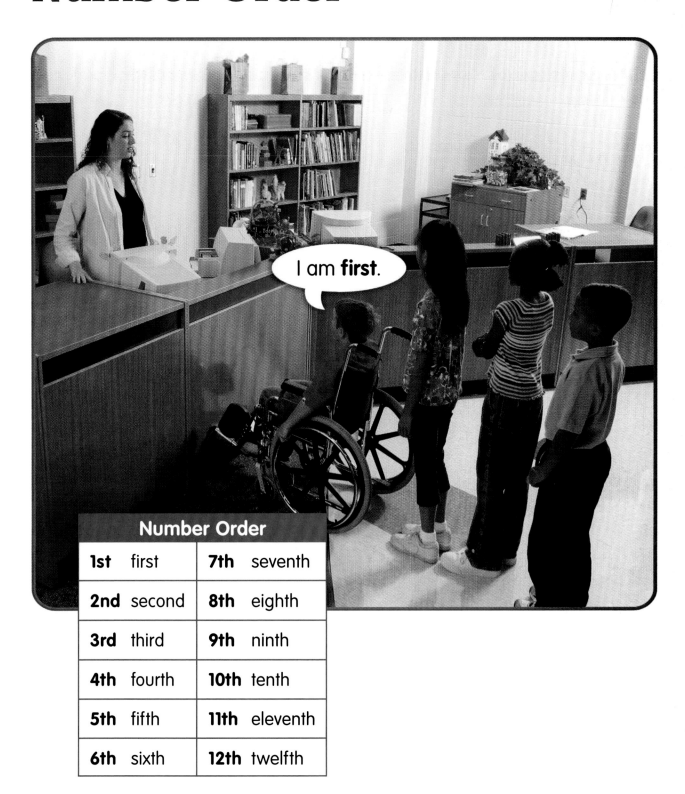

I am **first**.

Number Order

1st	first	**7th**	seventh
2nd	second	**8th**	eighth
3rd	third	**9th**	ninth
4th	fourth	**10th**	tenth
5th	fifth	**11th**	eleventh
6th	sixth	**12th**	twelfth

Say Hello

When You Greet a Friend

When You Greet an Adult

Say Good-bye

When You Say Good-bye to a Friend

Bye!

See you later.

See you tomorrow!

So long!

When You Say Good-bye to an Adult

Good-bye. I'll see you tomorrow.

Good-bye, Mrs. Park!

Have a nice afternoon!

Thank you. Good-bye now.

Say Thank You

Meet New People

Ask for Help

Just the Right Word

flag

buildings

trees

fountain

people

In Your Community

doctor's office

bakery

Park Drive

Words That Tell Where

The police station is **on** Main Street.

Main Street

The gas station is **next to** the police station.

The movie theater is **across from** the gas station.

The bakery is **below** the doctor's office.

The doctor's office is **above** the bakery.

The police station is **between** the gas station and the supermarket.

Community Workers

The **farmer** works on a **farm**.

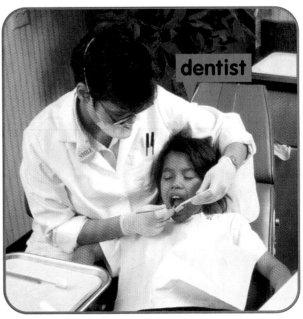

The **dentist** works in a **clinic**.

Who works in your community?

The **cashier** works in a **store**.

The **waiter** works in a **restaurant**.

The **judge** works in a **courtroom**.

The **firefighter** works in a **fire station**.

The **police officer** works all around the community.

Doctor's Office

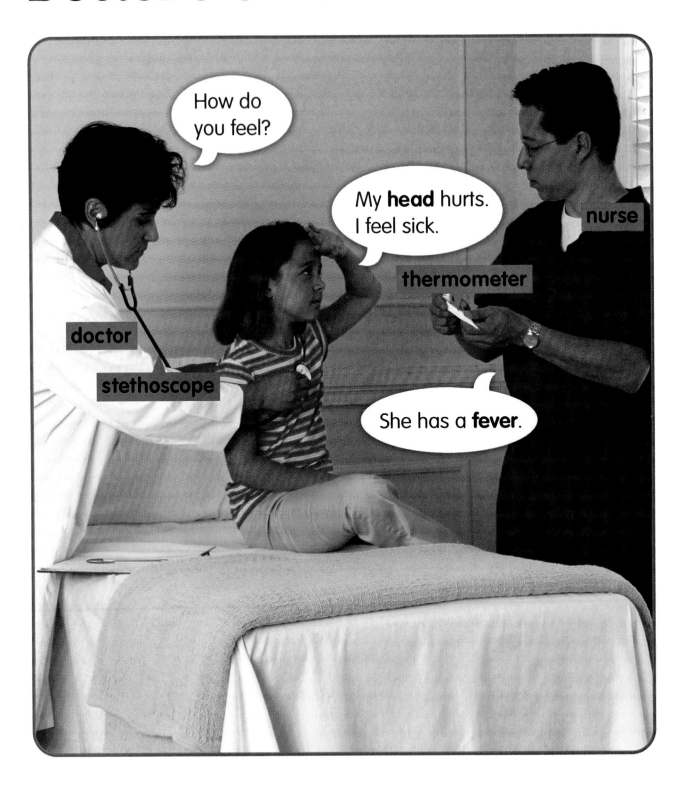

Just the Right Word

Your Body

hair
head
eye
nose
ear
mouth
throat
shoulder
arm
elbow
stomach
hand
finger
knee
leg
ankle
foot
toe

She has a
sore throat.

He has a
stomachache.

She has a
headache.

Just the Right Word

Transportation

taxicab

into the **tunnel**

over the **bridge**

around the **corner**

Just the Right Word 63

Signs and Safety

A hospital is near.

Cars have to stop here.

Slow down! Here is a school.

Cars cross the train tracks here.

People can cross the street here.

Here is the boys' bathroom.

Use this door to go outside.

Time

Days of the Week

There are seven days in a week.

month

NOVEMBER

days of the week

SUNDAY	MONDAY	TUESDAY	WEDNESDAY	THURSDAY	FRIDAY	SATURDAY
1	2	3	4	5	6	7
8	9	10	11	12	13	14
15	16	17	18	19	20	21
22	23	24	25	26	27	28
29	30					

date

Months

There are twelve months in a year.

January	April	July	October
February	May	August	November
March	June	September	December

Seasons

There are four seasons in a year.

spring

summer

autumn or **fall**

winter

Telling Time

It is **eight o'clock**.
It is time **for school**.

It is **twelve-thirty**.
It is time **for lunch**.

It is **quarter to three**.
It is time **to go home**.

It is **four forty-five**.
It is time **to do homework**.

It is **six fifteen**.
It is time **for dinner**.

It is **half-past eight**.
It is time **for bed**.

First, I go to school.
Then, I eat lunch. Later, I come home.
I do homework before dinner.
I go to bed after dinner.

clock

alarm clock

watch

Weather

umbrella

Spring is here! It is **warm** and **rainy**.

jacket

boots

It is **hot** and **sunny**. I love summer!

T-shirt

shorts

sandals

Words! Words! Words!

talk

pretty

happy

cold

Synonyms

Synonyms are words that mean almost the same thing.

angry

mad

upset

bothered

bad

awful

terrible

horrible

big

large

huge

enormous

cold

icy

chilly

freezing

go

move

walk

leave

good

great

terrific

fine

happy

glad

pleased

cheerful

like

enjoy

admire

love

little

small

tiny

wee

pretty

lovely

beautiful

cute

shout

scream

yell

holler

talk

speak

tell

say

Antonyms

Antonyms are words that have opposite meanings.

in   out

up   down

big   little

stop   go

cold   hot

good   bad

fast   slow   day   night

new   old   empty   full

happy   sad   clean   dirty

Compound Words

A **compound word** is a word made up
of two smaller words.

backpack
back + pack

baseball
base + ball

bathtub
bath + tub

classroom
class + room

fingernail
finger + nail

flashlight
flash + light

hairbrush
hair + brush

keyboard
key + board

mailbox
mail + box

popcorn
pop + corn

rainbow
rain + bow

sailboat
sail + boat

sidewalk
side + walk

waterfall
water + fall

Suffixes

A **suffix** is a word part that comes at the **end** of a word. A suffix changes the meaning of the word.

Suffixes	Examples
-able means "can be"	washable readable
-er means "a person who"	swimmer teacher
-ful means "full of"	helpful careful
-less means "without"	fearless colorless
-ly means "in a way that is"	quietly quickly

2+6=8

teacher

Prefixes

A **prefix** is a word part that comes at the
beginning of a word. A prefix changes
the meaning of the word.

Prefixes	Examples
dis- means "the opposite of"	disappear dislike
im-, in- mean "not"	imperfect incorrect
pre- means "before"	preview prewrite
re- means "again"	refill recycle
un- means "not"	unhappy uncomfortable

recycle

Multiple-Meaning Words

Multiple-meaning words look the same but have different meanings.

bank

The woman works at a **bank**.

The land on the side of a river is its **bank**.

bark

The dog can **bark**.

Trees have **bark**.

bat

Hit the ball with the **bat**.

A **bat** can fly.

jam

I put **jam** on my toast.

The cars are in a traffic **jam**.

leaves

Roy **leaves** the room.

The **leaves** fall off the tree.

train

Amalia can **train** her dog.

We ride the **train**.

turn

The dancer **turns** slowly.

We take **turns**.

Sound-Alike Words

Sound-alike words have the same sound when you say them, but they have different spellings and different meanings.

blue
blew

The butterfly is **blue**.

The wind **blew**.

eight
ate

A spider has **eight** legs.

I **ate** a banana.

hole
whole

There is a **hole** in his sock.

We ate the **whole** pizza.

sail
sale

The **sail** is white.

The store has a **sale**.

son
sun

The man has a **son**.

The **sun** is hot.

won
one

They **won** the game.

I have **one** pencil.

write
right

I **write** a story.

He raises his **right** hand.

Chapter 2
Picture It!

How are ideas connected? What do the parts of a story look like?

Use a picture to help you think about what you read and write.

First:

Next:

Then:

Last:

Charts

Charts show information.
They have rows and columns.

- Go down to read a column (⬇).
- Go across to read a row (➡).

column ⬇

Pets in My Neighborhood

Pets	Names
cat	Fluffy
fish	Blinky
dog	Nick

row ➡

Pets Owned by My Class

Pets	Total
Dogs	8
Cats	6
Hamsters	2
Birds	3
Guinea Pigs	1
Total Number of Pets	20

KWL Chart

A **KWL chart** helps you think about something as you study it. Read the question at the top of each column. It tells you how to complete the chart.

Topic: Pet Cats		
K **What Do I Know?**	**W** **What Do I Want to Learn?**	**L** **What Did I Learn?**
• Cats like to eat fish. • Cats like to play. • Cats sleep a lot.	• What should cats eat and drink? • Do cats need baths?	• Cats should eat special food that is made for cats. • Cats need fresh, clean water every day. • Milk is not good for cats. • Cats keep themselves clean.

Clusters

A **cluster** is a picture that shows how words or ideas go together.

Web

A cluster is sometimes called a **web**.

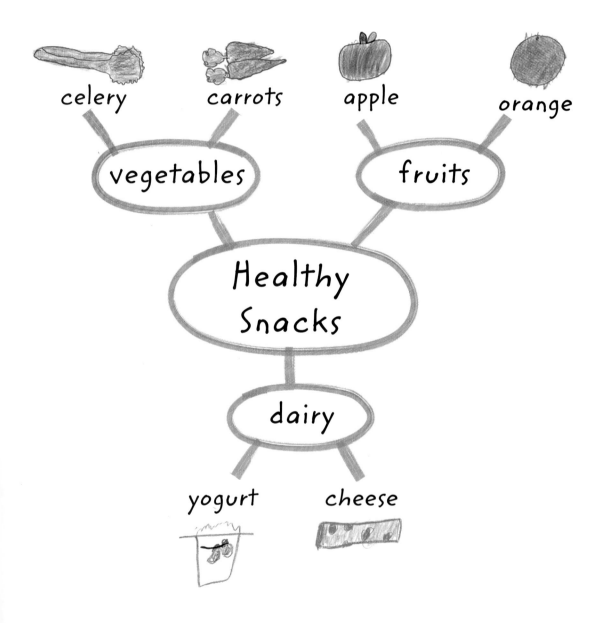

Picture It!

Character Map

A cluster is sometimes called a **map**. This map tells about a story character.

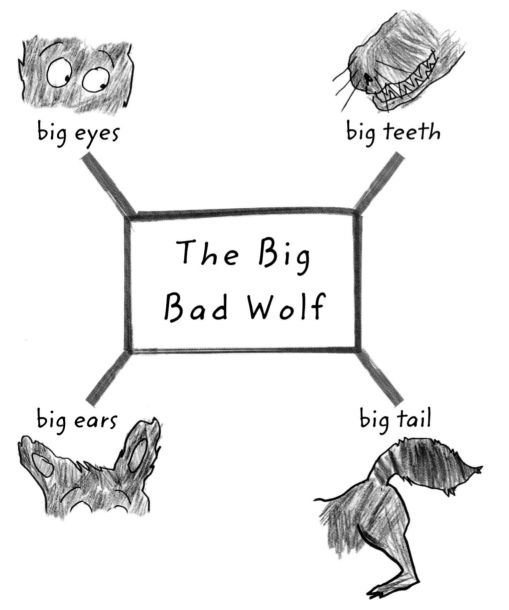

big eyes

big teeth

The Big Bad Wolf

big ears

big tail

Diagrams

A **diagram** is a picture that shows where things are, how something works, or how something happens. Words, or labels, give more information.

Parts Diagram

A **parts diagram** shows the **parts** of something. This diagram shows the parts of an oak tree.

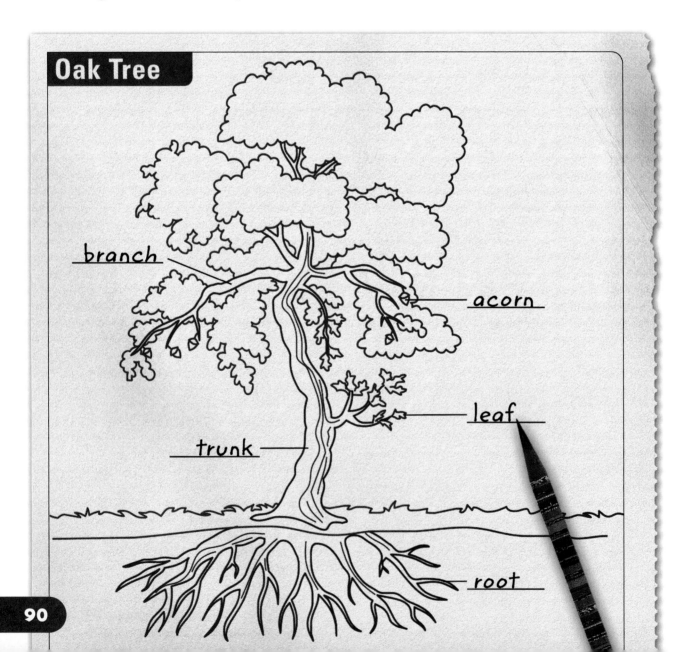

Oak Tree

branch

acorn

leaf

trunk

root

Process Diagram

A **process diagram** shows how something changes.
This diagram shows how an oak tree grows from
an acorn to a full-grown tree.

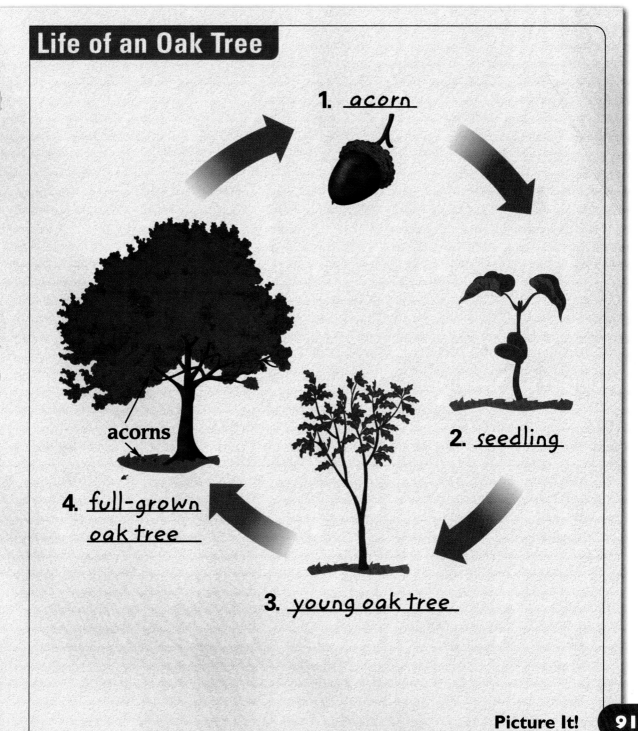

Life of an Oak Tree

1. _acorn_

2. _seedling_

3. _young oak tree_

4. _full-grown oak tree_

acorns

Venn Diagram

A **Venn diagram** shows how two things are the same and how they are different.

On this side, tell about one thing.

On this side, tell about the other thing.

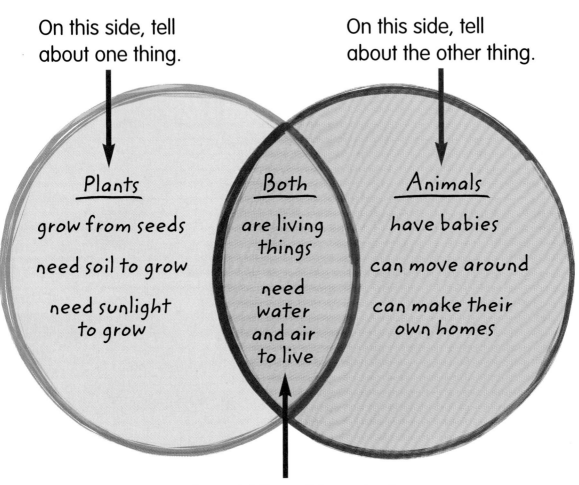

Plants

grow from seeds

need soil to grow

need sunlight to grow

Both

are living things

need water and air to live

Animals

have babies

can move around

can make their own homes

In the middle, tell how both things are the same.

Main Idea Diagram

A **main idea diagram** shows how details are related to a main idea.

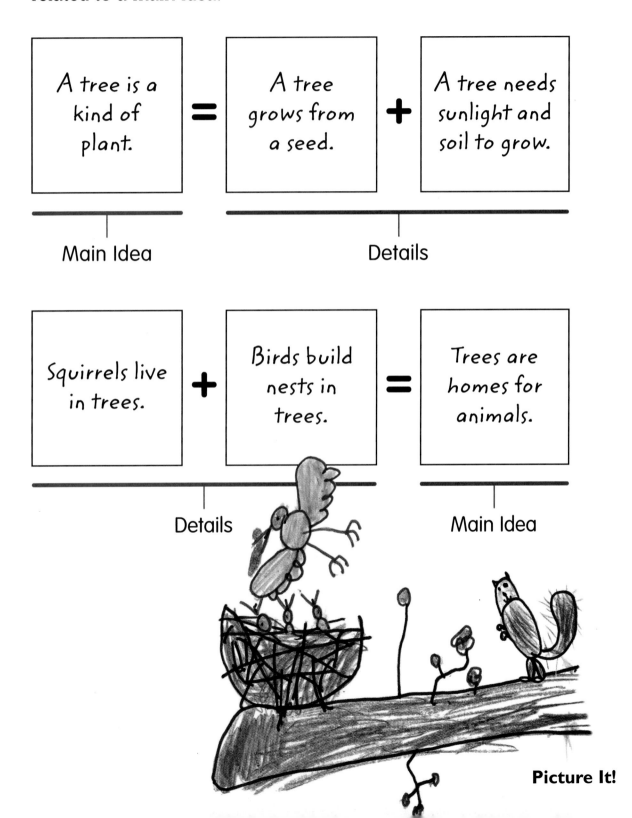

| A tree is a kind of plant. | = | A tree grows from a seed. | + | A tree needs sunlight and soil to grow. |

Main Idea   Details

| Squirrels live in trees. | + | Birds build nests in trees. | = | Trees are homes for animals. |

Details   Main Idea

Graphs

A **graph** is a drawing that gives information about how many or how much there are of something.

Bar Graph

A **bar graph** uses bars to show how many or how much.

Picture It!

Line Graph

A **line graph** has dots. Each dot shows how many there are of something at a certain time. The dots are connected by lines.

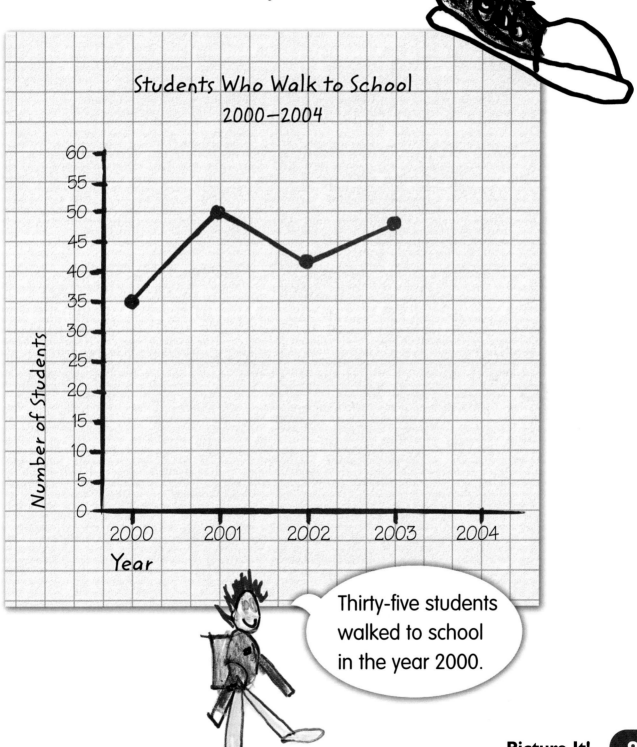

Students Who Walk to School 2000–2004

Number of Students

Year

Thirty-five students walked to school in the year 2000.

Pie Graph

A **pie graph** is round like a pie. It is divided into parts. Each part is a **percentage** of the whole pie. This graph shows how many students at a school like each sport.

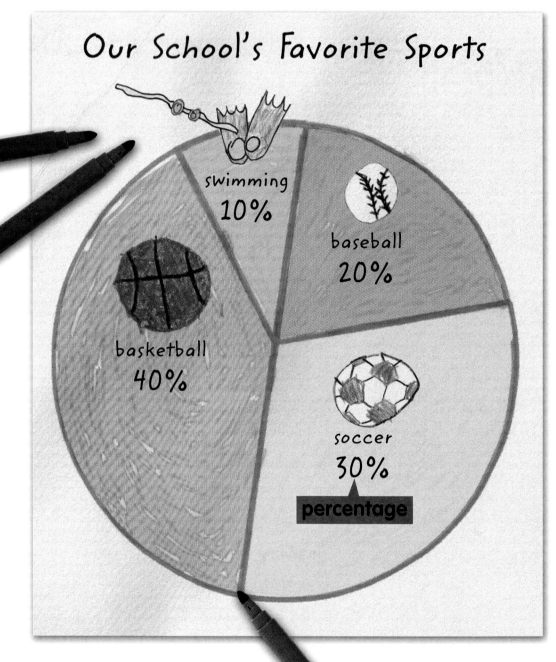

Our School's Favorite Sports

swimming 10%

baseball 20%

basketball 40%

soccer 30%

percentage

When you add up the **percentages**, they equal **100 percent**, or the whole pie.

Map

A **map** is a picture of a place. This map shows the United States. The **key** shows what each **symbol**, or picture, on the map means.

Story Maps

A **story map** tells about the parts of a story.

Character, Setting, and Plot

A story map can show these things:

- the **characters**, or who is in the story
- the **setting**, or where the story happens
- the **plot**, or what happens in the story.

Title: _Anansi and Turtle_

Character:
Turtle

Setting:
The woods and the river

Character:
Anansi the Spider

Plot:

Turtle visits Anansi in the woods.
Anansi does not want to share his dinner with Turtle.
So he plays a trick on Turtle.
The trick helps Anansi keep his dinner.

Months later, Anansi visits Turtle in the river.
This time, Turtle plays a trick on Anansi.
The trick helps Turtle keep his own dinner.

Beginning, Middle, and End

This story map tells what happens in each part of the story.

Title: _The Ants and the Grasshopper_

Beginning

The ants gather food all summer. They store it for the winter. The grasshopper sings and plays.

⬇

Middle

The ants warn the grasshopper to save food for himself. But the grasshopper does not want to work. When winter comes, the grasshopper is cold and hungry.

⬇

End

The ants feel sorry for the grasshopper. They share their food with him. Then the grasshopper plays music for the ants.

Sequence Chain

This story map shows the order, or **sequence**, in which story events happen.

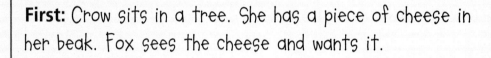

Title: The Fox and the Crow

Author: Aesop

First: Crow sits in a tree. She has a piece of cheese in her beak. Fox sees the cheese and wants it.

↓

Next: Fox tells Crow that she is beautiful. He says she must have a beautiful voice, too. Fox asks Crow to sing.

↓

Then: Crow opens her beak to sing and drops the cheese.

↓

Last: Fox catches the cheese and eats it!

Problem-and-Solution Map

Some stories are all about a **problem** and how the problem gets solved, or its **solution**.

Title: The Crowded House

Characters: a farmer, his wife and children, and a wise man
Setting: a one-room house

↓

Problem: A farmer lives in a one-room house with his wife and six children. It is too crowded.

↓

Event 1: The farmer asks a wise man for help. The wise man tells the farmer to bring the pigs and the chickens into the house.

Event 2: Now the house is very crowded. The wise man tells the farmer to bring the other animals into the house.

Event 3: Now the house is full! There is no more room. The wise man tells the farmer to take all the animals out of the house.

↓

Solution: The farmer thinks the house is not crowded anymore.

Goal-and-Outcome Map

In some stories, a character tries to reach a **goal**. The goal is what the character tries to get or do, or where the character wants to go. The **outcome** is what happens at the end.

Title: _The Fox in the Moon_

Author: _Juan Quintana_

Goal:

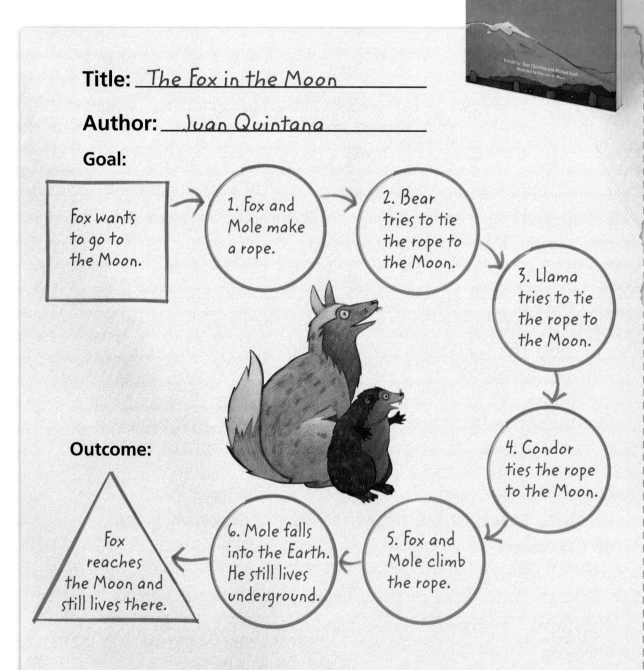

Fox wants to go to the Moon.

1. Fox and Mole make a rope.

2. Bear tries to tie the rope to the Moon.

3. Llama tries to tie the rope to the Moon.

4. Condor ties the rope to the Moon.

5. Fox and Mole climb the rope.

6. Mole falls into the Earth. He still lives underground.

Outcome:

Fox reaches the Moon and still lives there.

Picture It!

Cause-and-Effect Map

A **cause-and-effect map** shows the events in a story and why they happen.

Title: <u>Two of Everything</u>

Author: <u>Lily Toy Hong</u>

Cause	Effect
Mr. Haktak finds a brass pot. He puts his purse with five gold coins into the pot.	He finds two purses with five gold coins each inside the pot.
Mrs. Haktak's hairpin falls into the pot.	She finds two hairpins in the pot.
Mr. Haktak puts his winter coat into the pot.	He finds two winter coats in the pot.
The Haktaks put coins into the pot.	The pot is filled with coins.
Mrs. Haktak falls into the pot. Mr. Haktak falls into the pot.	Now there are two Mrs. Haktaks and two Mr. Haktaks.

Time Lines

A **time line** lists when important events happen. It tells about each event in the order that it happened. This time line shows special events in a person's life. Read it from left to right (➡).

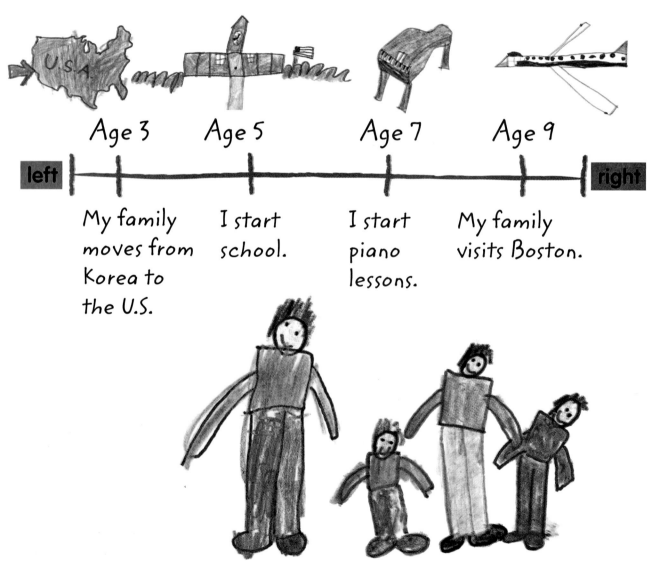

Age 3   Age 5   Age 7   Age 9

left   **right**

My family moves from Korea to the U.S.

I start school.

I start piano lessons.

My family visits Boston.

This time line tells about inventions.
Read it from top to bottom (⬇).

top

Inventions

 1876
Alexander Graham Bell
invents the telephone.

 1879
Thomas Edison invents
the electric lightbulb.

 1908
Henry Ford invents the
Model T car.

 1923
Garrett A. Morgan
invents the traffic light.

 1927
Philo Farnsworth
invents the television.

 1945
The first electronic
computer is invented.

bottom

Chapter 3
Put It in Writing!

I think it is good to play sport

What do you want to tell people?
How do you want to say it?

Just follow the steps to put your ideas in writing.

I think it is important to play a sport. Sports are good for your health. When you run, kick, and jump, you get a lot of exercise. You learn new tricks. If you are on a team, you can make new friends. Sports make you feel good about yourself, even if you do not win!

The Writing Process

The **Writing Process** has five steps. Follow these steps to make your writing better.

1 Prewrite

Plan what you will write.

■ **Think of ideas.** Make a list or draw pictures. Collect your ideas in a writing file.

Our Street Fair

■ **Choose an idea.** Look at your writing file. Which idea do you like best? Choose one. This will be your **topic.**

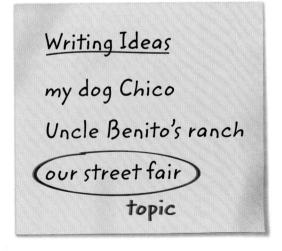

Writing Ideas

my dog Chico

Uncle Benito's ranch

our street fair
topic

■ Choose your purpose, audience, and form.

Ask yourself these questions. They will help
you decide how to write about your topic.

1. Why are you writing? This is your **purpose**.

2. Who is going to read your writing? This is
    your **audience**.

3. What are you writing? This is your **form**.

You can make an **FATP** chart to help you remember.

Form:	A description
Audience:	My classmates
Topic:	The street fair
Purpose:	To describe something

I will write a
description to tell
my class about
the street fair.

Prewrite, continued

■ **Think about what you know.** What do you
already know about your topic? Collect details.
Here are two ways.

• You can make a **cluster**.

• You can make a **5Ws chart**.

TOPIC: Our Street Fair	
Who?	neighbors, Mrs. Vega, Mr. Guerra
What?	games, food, music, dancing, stories
When?	last week
Where?	my street
Why?	fun!

■ **Organize your details.** A **diagram** is one way to organize details. It can help you decide what order to use when you write.

Topic: Our Street Fair — Write your topic here.

1. music, danced
2. piñata
3. Mrs. Vega's tamales — List your details in order.
4. Mr. Guerra told stories

Mr. Guerra told stories after we ate. I will put that detail last.

② Draft

When you write your **first draft**, you turn ideas
into sentences. You use the sentences to make paragraphs.
Write your draft quickly. You can correct mistakes later.

■ Write a **topic sentence** to tell the main idea
　of a paragraph.

Topic: Our Street Fair ——— Our street fair made
everyone smile!

■ Write more sentences to add the **details**.

Topic: Our Street Fair

1. music, danced
2. piñata

Our street fair made
everyone smile! There
was music. People danced
and danced. We had a
piñata.

Keys to the Computer

You can use the computer to **write your draft**.

monitor

Document 1

Our street fair made everyone smile! There was music. People danced and danced. We had a piñata. There were so many kinds of food. Mrs. Vega's tamales were the best!

screen

The **cursor** shows where you are.

Press **delete** to take something away.

Press **tab** to indent a paragraph.

keyboard

Press **shift** and a **letter key** to make a capital letter.

Press the **space bar** to make a **space** between words.

Press **return** to start a new line.

Use the **mouse** to move the cursor.

❸ Revise

When you **revise**, you make changes.
They make your writing better and clearer.

■ Read your draft. Ask yourself these questions:

✓ Did I say what I wanted to say?

✓ Are the sentences in the right order?

✓ Will my readers understand?

✓ Is my writing interesting?

> Maybe I should say exactly how the tamales tasted.

Our street fair made everyone smile!
There was music. People danced and danced.
We had a piñata. There were so many kinds
of food. Mrs. Vega's tamales were the best!
The kids also got to play a lot of games.
And then we listened to Mr. Guerra's stories.

> Is this detail about the piñata in the right place?

> I need to say more about Mr. Guerra's stories.

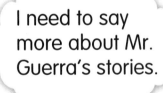

■ Have a partner read your draft two times. Discuss your draft in a **peer conference**.

The reader should:	The writer should:
Say what the writing is about. Tell what you like best.	Listen carefully.
Ask questions. Tell how to make the writing better.	Think about your partner's ideas.

This is about a street fair. I like the part about tamales.

Can you add more details about the music?

Good idea! I'll tell more about the salsa band.

Revising, continued

■ Make your changes. Use the **revising marks**.

Revising Marks

Mark	Meaning
∧	Add.
⌣	Take out.
∧	Change to this.
⌣	Move to here.

These details give a clearer picture.

This sentence is out of order. It belongs with games.

Now my readers will know how the tamales tasted.

Our street fair made everyone smile!

A band played salsa   All the neighbors

There was music. People danced and danced.

We had a piñata. There were so many kinds

spicy

of food. Mrs. Vega's tamales were the best!

The kids also got to play a lot of games.

And then we listened to Mr. Guerra's stories.

STEP

4 Edit and Proofread

When you **edit and proofread**, you look for mistakes.
When you find a mistake, fix it. Follow these steps:

1. Read your writing.

2. Make sure words are spelled correctly.

3. Look for mistakes in capitalization, grammar, and punctuation.

4. Use **proofreading marks** to show what you need to fix.

Proofreading Marks

Mark	Meaning
∧	Add.
∧,	Add a comma.
⊙	Add a period.
≡	Capitalize.
◯	Check spelling.
/	Make lowercase.
~~	Take out.

The kids also got to play a lot of games. We had a piñata. ~~And~~ then we listened to Mr. Guerra's stories. They were funny. He made his voice sound like different Animals. His bear voice really made us laff.

Keys to the Computer

If you write on the computer, you can also use it to **check your spelling**. Follow these steps to check the spelling of all the words in your writing:

STEP
1 Click on **Tools** in the toolbar. You will see a menu.

STEP
2 Click on **Spelling** in the menu. The computer will show misspelled words in color.

Put It in Writing!

STEP

3 The computer will show you a list of **suggestions**. Click on the word you want.

STEP

4 Click on the **Change** button. This corrects the spelling of the word in your writing.

The word **laff** was changed to **laugh**.

He made his voice sound like different animals. His bear voice really made us laugh .

Put It in Writing! 119

⑤ Publish

To **publish** means to present, or show, your work.
You make a final copy of your writing. Then you
share it. You can:

- Read your work out loud to
  a classmate.

- E-mail your work to a family member
  or friend.

- Turn your work into a book.

- Turn your work into a play. Act it out.

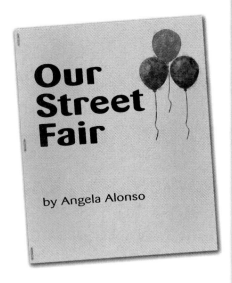

Our Street Fair
by Angela Alonso

Our street fair made everyone smile!
A band played salsa music. All the neighbors
danced and danced. There were many kinds
of food. Mrs. Vega's spicy tamales were
the best!

The kids also got to play a lot of games.
We had a piñata. Then we listened to
Mr. Guerra's stories. They were funny. He
made his voice sound like different animals.
His bear voice really made us laugh.

Keys to the Computer

You can use the computer and a **printer** to **publish your writing**. Follow these steps:

on/off button

printer

paper tray

1. Turn on the printer. Make sure there is paper in the **paper tray**.

2. Click on **File** in the computer toolbar. Click on **Print** in the menu.

File	Edit	Format	Tools
New ...
Open ...
Close
Save
Save As
Print
Quit

3. How many **copies** do you want? Type a number in the box. Click on **Print** to start printing.

number

| File | Edit | Format | Tools |

Printer: Las   Destination: Printer

General

Copies: 3   ☐ Collated

Pages: ● All
       ○ From: ___ To: ___

Paper Source: ● All pages from: Auto Select
              ○ First page from: Cassette (Standard)

Save Settings   Cancel   Print

Kinds of Writing

Announcement

An **announcement** is a short message. It tells about a special event, such as a play, festival, or other fun activity.

Tell what the event is.

Tell **when** and **where** the event will be.

Give details.

FAMILY FUN NIGHT

Friday, October 12
7:00–8:00 p.m.
At Long Hill School

Come for stories, games, music, and more!
Bring the whole family!

Book Review

Do you want to tell about a book you read? Then write a **book review**.

My Review of <u>Dear Juno</u>

Tell the title of the book. Underline the title.

Name the author.

<u>Dear Juno</u> is a book by Soyung Pak. It tells about a boy named Juno who lives in the United States. Juno writes letters to his grandmother.

She lives in Korea. Grandmother writes back in Korean, but Juno cannot read it! Then Grandmother sends photos. They help Juno understand.

Tell what the book is about.

I like this book because it tells about ways that people can share the important things in their lives. The book has beautiful pictures, too!

Did you like the book? Tell why or why not.

Description

A **description** tells what someone or something is like.

Description of a Person

You can describe a real or made-up person. Use words that help your reader "see" the person.

Name the person.

Tell what the person looks like. Use **describing words**.

Tell about the person's **actions**.

What is special or interesting about the person? Give **details** and **examples**.

My Best Friend

My best friend is Theo. He has dark hair and brown eyes. He is smaller than me, but he can run faster!

Theo likes to build things. He likes to help people learn things, too. Theo showed me how to build a model airplane. Now we are building a clubhouse together.

Description of a Place

You can describe a real or made-up place. Use details to help your readers "see" the place.

Name the place in the **topic sentence**.

Use **sensory words** to tell how things look, sound, feel, smell, or taste.

Use **location words** to tell where things are.

My Uncle's Garden

My uncle's garden looks like a rainbow. Uncle Luis grows all kinds of vegetables and fruits there. He has smooth, green watermelons and bright yellow peppers. He grows red, juicy tomatoes. There are small, pink flowers all around the garden. That's why his garden smells so sweet.

My uncle's garden is noisy, too. Bees buzz in and out of the flowers. Birds chirp and sing above my head. I love to listen to my uncle's garden!

Directions

Some **directions** tell how to make something. Others tell how to get to a place. Always put the steps in your directions in order.

How to Make Something

Maracas

YOU WILL NEED:
▶ 2 small, clean plastic bottles with caps
▶ small seeds, beads, or stones
▶ paint

The list of **materials** tells you what to use.

❶ Pour a handful of seeds, stones, or beads into two plastic bottles.

❷ Screw the bottle caps onto the bottles.

❸ Paint the bottles. Now you have maracas!

❹ Hold the maracas by the necks. Shake them to make your music!

The **steps** have numbers to show the order.

23 KIDS' CRAFTS

How to Get to a Place

Use **direction words**. They tell people which way to go.

Add **details** to describe the place so that people can find it.

Draw a map. It helps people see where to go.

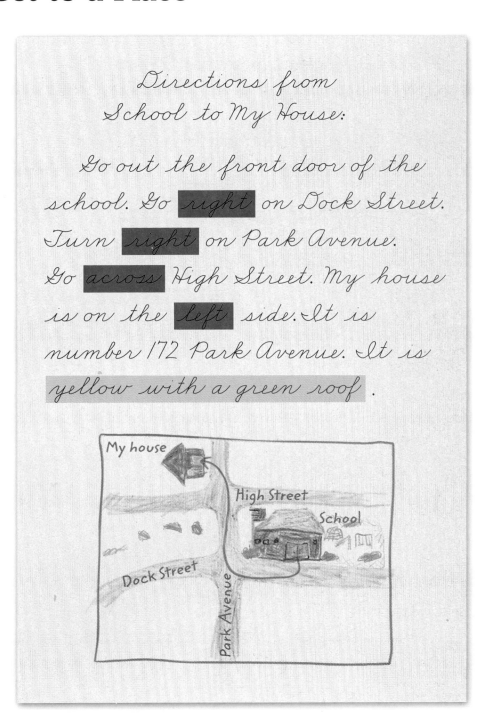

Directions from
School to My House:

Go out the front door of the school. Go **right** on Dock Street. Turn **right** on Park Avenue. Go **across** High Street. My house is on the **left** side. It is number 172 Park Avenue. It is **yellow with a green roof**.

My house

High Street

School

Dock Street

Park Avenue

E-mail

E-mail is a message you send by computer. "E-mail" is a shorter way to say **electronic mail**. You can send e-mail to anyone who has an e-mail address.

An **attachment** is a picture or other file. Click here to add an attachment.

Click on **Send** to send the message.

Type your friend's e-mail address here.

Type what your message is about.

Type your message here.

This is the **attachment**. Your friend will click on it to open it.

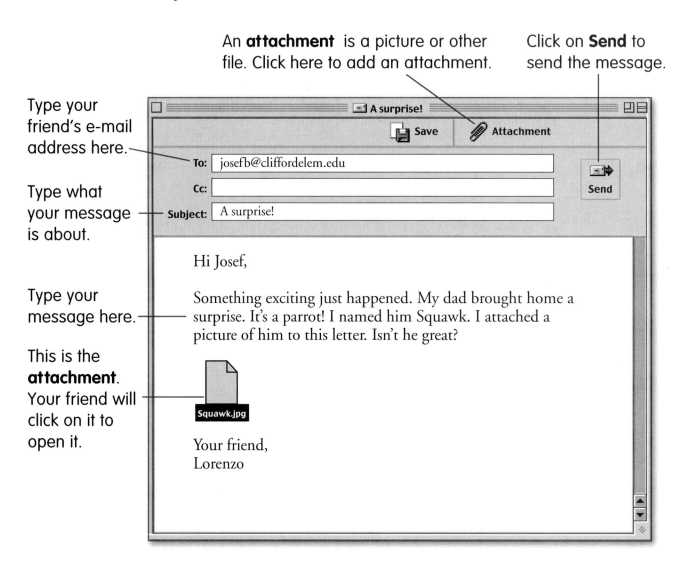

Put It in Writing!

Fable

A **fable** is a story with a lesson, or **moral**. The moral tells what you can learn from the story.

The Ant and the Bird
A Fable by Aesop

An ant and a bird lived in the woods near a stream. One day, the ant wanted a drink. She fell into the stream! The water carried her away.

The bird saw what happened. He dropped a leaf into the stream. Then he yelled, "Crawl onto the leaf!"

The ant crawled onto the leaf. She floated safely to dry land.

Soon, a man came to the woods. He set a trap to catch the bird. The ant stung the man's foot. The man yelled loudly. The bird heard the noise and flew safely away.

Moral: When someone does something nice for you, do something nice back.

The **characters** are often animals. They talk and act like people.

The **moral** comes at the end of the story.

Journal Entry

A **journal** is a special book that you keep for yourself. Each time you write in it, you create a **journal entry**.

Begin with the **date**.

October 16, 2003

Write about what happened to you.

Today Ms. Sims asked us to draw pictures of our favorite things. I drew a dolphin. I thought my picture looked great! Ms. Sims must think it looks great, too. She put it on the wall with a few others. I felt excited and proud. I might draw some more sea animals now, because I like them so much.

Tell about your thoughts and feelings.

Labels and Captions

A **label** names something in a picture.
A **caption** tells more about a picture.

Animal Homes

label ►nest

caption ► The bird lives in a nest.

den

The fox lives in a den.

Letters and Notes

Friendly Letter

You can write a **friendly letter** to someone you know well.

Write your address and the date. This is the **heading**.

8 Red Bird Way
Sacramento, CA 95829
September 9, 2003

Write your friend's name in the greeting.

Dear Ming,

  I can't believe I have already lived here for two weeks! I like my new school. My teacher asked me to bring in some things that tell about myself. I brought in pictures of you and me at the Golden Dragon parade last year. Now my classmates want to make a giant dragon!

  How is everything in San Francisco? Tell everyone I say hi!

In the **body**, tell your news. Ask questions.

Write a closing and **sign your name**.

Your friend,
Jin-nah

Envelope

Put your letter in an **envelope**. Write neatly. Check everything carefully. This will help your letter get to the right place!

Write your name and address here. This is the **return address**.

Jin-nah Yang
8 Red Bird Way
Sacramento, CA 95829

Ming Lu
652 Docker Street
San Francisco, CA 94108

Put a **stamp** in the top right corner.

Write your friend's name and address here. This is the **mailing address**.

Invitation

An **invitation** asks someone to come to a party or other special event.

Tell **when** and **where** the event will take place.

Come to a Kwanzaa Dinner!

Enjoy a special night with family and friends.

Date: Saturday, January 1
Time: 6:30 p.m.
Place: Nikki's house
       239 Cook Street

R.S.V.P. 555-0931

R.S.V.P. means "Please respond." It asks people to call and say if they will come.

Thank–you Note

Send a **thank-you note** when someone gives you a gift or does something nice for you.

Write the **date**.

Write a **greeting**.

Say "thank you."
Tell why you
like the gift.

Write a **closing**.
Sign your name.

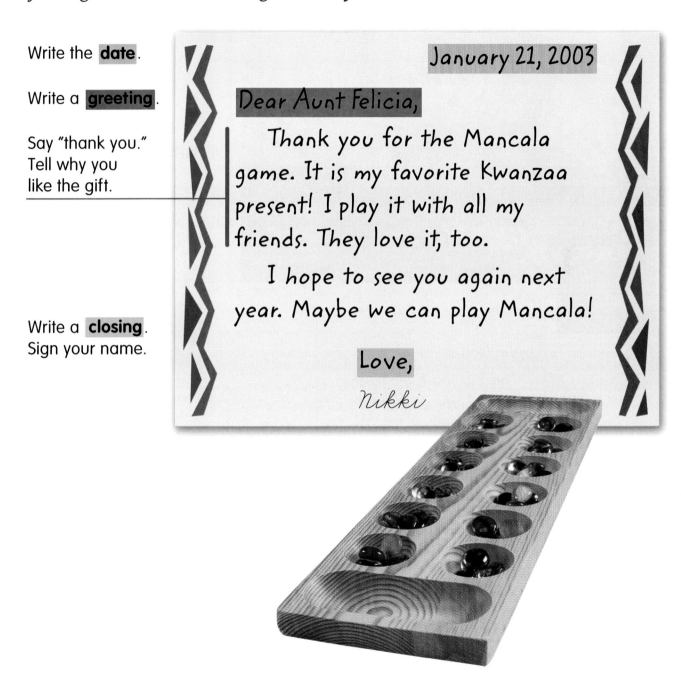

January 21, 2003

Dear Aunt Felicia,

   Thank you for the Mancala game. It is my favorite Kwanzaa present! I play it with all my friends. They love it, too.

   I hope to see you again next year. Maybe we can play Mancala!

Love,

Nikki

Postcard

When you go on a trip, send a **postcard** to your friends. It tells about your trip.

front

Put a **stamp** in the corner.

Write your **message** on the back.

April 3, 2002

Dear Nadia,

The Florida Everglades are wild! We saw some scary alligators. Tomorrow we are going to the beach. I hope there are no alligators there!

Your friend,
Alfonso

The Everglades National Park, Florida

Nadia Davidov
4225 South Street
York, PA 19042

Write your friend's **name and address** here.

back

List

A **list** can help you remember things.

Shopping List
eggs
flour
sugar
butter
milk

Message

A message is a short note. It tells someone something quickly. Here is a **telephone message**.

For whom is the message? Write the name.

Write the date.

Tell who called, when, and why.

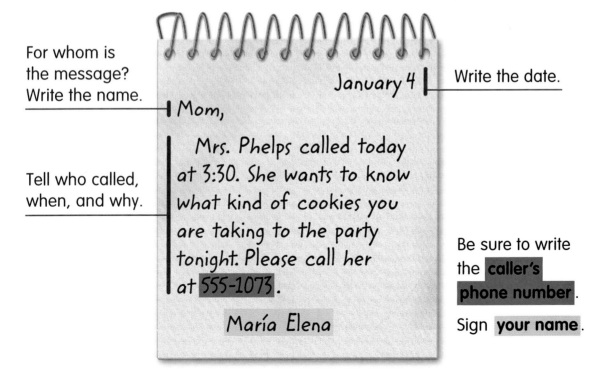

January 4

Mom,

Mrs. Phelps called today at 3:30. She wants to know what kind of cookies you are taking to the party tonight. Please call her at 555-1073.

María Elena

Be sure to write the **caller's phone number**.

Sign **your name**.

Newsletter

A **newsletter** gives information about a school, a club, or another group. Newsletters are often published once a week or once a month.

News Story

A newsletter can have a **news story**. It tells about an event that really happened. It includes **facts**.

The **headline** tells what the story is about.

Facts tell **who, what, when, where,** and **why**.

Pine Street School News

May 2003

Third Graders Clean Up!

by Yolanda Ortiz

Students in Mr. Soto's third-grade class helped clean up City Park last Saturday. They picked up litter and raked leaves. Some students planted flowers. Many parents and teachers helped, too.

Rochelle Lamar is one student who helped. She said, "We wanted to make the park clean and safe. We want it to look nice, too."

Mayor Romero thanked the students. She said, "These students show how we can all work together to make our city better."

Advertisement

A newsletter can have an **advertisement**, or **ad**. An ad tries to get people to buy something. It can include facts and opinions.

An **opinion** tells how someone feels about something.

A **fact** is true information.

Show your school pride!

BUY A PINE STREET T-SHIRT!

only $9.95

It's the coolest shirt in town!

Shirts come in:
small • medium • large

Pine Street Pride

Pine Street School News
May 2003

Third Graders Clean Up!
by Yolanda Ortiz

Students in Mr. Soto's third-grade class helped clean up City Park last Saturday. They picked up litter and raked leaves. Some students planted flowers. Many parents and teachers helped, too.

Rochelle Lamar is one student who helped. She said, "We wanted to make the park clean and safe. We want it to look nice, too."

Mayor Romero thanked the students. She said, "These students show how we can all work together to make our city better."

Show your school pride!
BUY A PINE STREET T-SHIRT!
only $9.95
It's the coolest shirt in town!
Shirts come in:
small • medium • large

Paragraph

A **paragraph** is a group of sentences. They all tell about the same idea. The topic sentence gives the **main idea**. The other sentences give **details** that support it.

A Paragraph with Examples

Some paragraphs give **examples** to support the main idea.

Start with a **topic sentence**. It tells the main idea.

Indent, or leave a space before the first word.

There are a lot of fun things to do at Jefferson City Park. You can swing on the swings. You can slide down the big slide. You can play basketball or baseball. You can even go to the lake and feed the ducks. That is my favorite thing to do!

Write detail sentences to give **examples**.

Sequence Paragraph

A **sequence paragraph** tells the order, or sequence, of several events. You can write a sequence paragraph to explain how you did something.

The **topic sentence** tells the main thing you did.

The detail sentences tell exactly what you did.

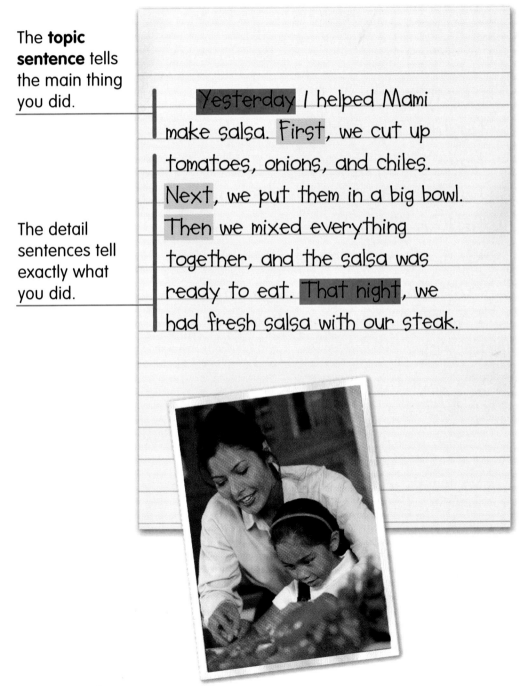

Yesterday I helped Mami make salsa. First, we cut up tomatoes, onions, and chiles. Next, we put them in a big bowl. Then we mixed everything together, and the salsa was ready to eat. That night, we had fresh salsa with our steak.

Use **time words** and **order words** to show the **sequence**.

A Paragraph That Compares

When you **compare**, you tell how two or more things are the same or different. You can write a paragraph to compare two people.

The **topic sentence** tells whom you are comparing.

Detail sentences tell how the people are **alike**.

Comparison words make your ideas clear.

My brother Elijah looks a lot like my father. They both have black, curly hair. Elijah has brown eyes just like my father. They have the same kind of smile, too! It is very cute. Sometimes I wish that I looked like my father and brother.

Opinion Paragraph

In an **opinion paragraph**, you give your thoughts and feelings about a topic.

The topic sentence gives your **opinion**.

> I think it is important to play a sport. Sports are good for your health. When you run, kick, and jump, you get a lot of exercise. You learn new tricks. If you are on a team, you can make new friends. Sports make you feel good about yourself, even if you do not win!

The detail sentences give **reasons** for your opinion.

Play

A **play** is a story that is acted out on stage. **Actors** take the roles of the characters. You watch what the actors do, and you listen to what they say.

The actors are performing the play *Annie* **on stage.**

People buy tickets at the **theater** to see the play.

The author of a play is called a **playwright**. The playwright writes the script.

Script for a Play

The **script** tells the actors what to say and do.
The actors use the script to **rehearse**, or practice,
their lines. Then they perform the play.

Annie

The script lists the **characters** and tells the **setting**.

Characters:

Annie, a young girl with no parents

Mr. Warbucks, a rich man

Grace, a woman who works for Mr. Warbucks

Miss Hannigan, a mean woman who runs the home where Annie lives

Other girls who live with Annie

Setting: *New York City in the 1930s*

A play often has **acts**. An act is like a chapter in a book. Each act has smaller parts, or **scenes**.

Act 2, Scene 3

Annie is at Mr. Warbucks' house with Grace.

Grace *(talking to Mr. Warbucks)*: This is Annie. She is the girl you wanted from the orphanage.

Annie: Hello, Mr. Warbucks! It's nice to meet you. *(She holds out her hand to shake his.)*

Mr. Warbucks: I wanted a boy, not a girl! You can't stay.

The script shows the **dialogue**, or the words the characters say. The **stage directions** *(in italics)* tell the actors what to do.

Poem

A **poem** uses words in a special way to give the reader a certain feeling.

Rhyming Poem

In a **rhyming poem**, some of the words **rhyme**, or have the same ending sound. The rhyming words have a **pattern**.

In a poem, a row of words is called a **line**.

Look at the **pattern** in this poem. The rhyming words come at the end of every two lines.

Rainy Day

I do not like a rainy day.

The road is wet, the sky is gray.

They dress me up, from head to toes,

In lots and lots of rubber clothes.

I wish the sun would come and stay.

I do not like a rainy day.

—William Wise

This poem has rhyming words with a different **pattern**.

Look at the words that **rhyme**. Look at the words that **do not rhyme**. Can you see the **pattern**?

Tommy

I put a seed into the ground
And said, "I'll watch it grow."
I watered it and cared for it
As well as I could know.

One day I walked in my back yard,
And oh, what did I see!
My seed had popped itself right out,
Without consulting me.

—*Gwendolyn Brooks*

Put It in Writing! 147

Limerick

A **limerick** is a funny poem with five lines. It has a special pattern. Lines 1, 2, and 5 rhyme one way. Lines 3 and 4 rhyme another way. Lines 1 and 5 sometimes end with the same word.

Chin and **pin** rhyme. **Sharp** and **harp** rhyme.

Lines 3 and 4 are shorter than the others. This gives the poem its **rhythm**, or beat.

There was a young lady whose chin,

Resembled the point of a pin.

So she had it made sharp,

And purchased a harp,

And played several tunes with her chin.

—Edward Lear

Poem with Sound Words

Some poems have words that sound like what they mean. For example, the word **buzz** sounds like the noise a fly makes. These words are called sound words, or **onomatopoeia**.

Say some of the **sound words** out loud. Do they sound like the things they tell about?

Ears Hear

Flies buzz,
Motors roar.
Kettles hiss,
People snore.
Dogs bark,
Birds cheep.
Autos honk: *Beep! Beep!*

Kids shout,
Clocks ding.
Babies cry,
Phones ring.
Balls bounce,
Spoons drop.
People scream: *Stop! Stop!*

—Lucia and James L. Hymes, Jr.

Story

Writers use their imagination to make up stories.
These stories are called **fiction**.

- Every story has **characters**. They are the people or animals in the story. In most stories, the characters speak. Their words are called **dialogue**.

May we go to the beach today?

Yes, that's a great idea!

Stan and his mother

park rangers

- Every story happens in a certain place and time. This is called the **setting**.

the beach on Saturday

- Every story has a **plot**. The plot tells what events happen in the **beginning**, **middle**, and **end** of a story.

beginning

middle

end

Realistic Fiction

Realistic fiction tells about events that can really happen.

Stan and his mother went to the beach on Saturday. They saw a baby whale. It was almost up to the beach.

"We have to help the baby whale!" cried Stan. "It must be lost!"

Stan and his mom called the park rangers. The rangers came with a raft. They worked for a long time. Finally the rangers got the baby whale away from shore. The whale swam out to sea.

Stan was happy. "I bet that little whale will be glad to see his mother," said Stan. He hugged his own mother tightly.

The characters and **setting** seem real. These **events** could really happen.

These **events** could really happen.

Fantasy

A **fantasy** is a story about things that could never happen in real life.

RABBIT, COYOTE, AND THE BIG ROCK

A Folk Tale from Guatemala

One day, Rabbit was leaning on a big rock when Coyote came by. Rabbit decided to play a trick on Coyote.

"What are you doing?" Coyote asked Rabbit.

"Help me, Coyote! The sky is falling on us! Lean against this rock to hold up the sky. I'll go get a stick," said Rabbit. "We can use it to keep the rock up."

"All right," said Coyote. He leaned against

In real life, animals cannot talk. In this **fantasy**, Rabbit and Coyote talk to each other.

the rock with all his might.

Rabbit ran off and left Coyote holding up the rock. After a while, Coyote shouted, "Hurry up, Rabbit! I'm getting very tired." Rabbit did not come back.

A little later, Coyote cried, "Rabbit, WHERE ARE YOU? I can't hold up this rock any longer!" Rabbit still did not come back. Finally Coyote decided to leave. "I don't care if the sky falls down," he said.

As Coyote was running away, he fell into a ravine! That's how Coyote was lost forever, and Rabbit never did come back.

In a **fantasy**, the characters often do things they cannot do in real life. Here Coyote holds up a rock.

A Story About You

You can write a story about something that happened to you. This kind of story is called a **personal narrative**.

Use **I**, **me** and **my**. They show that the story is about you.

My Visit to Japan

When **I** was three years old, **my** family moved to the U.S. from Japan. This year, my parents took **me** back to Japan for the first time. I was very excited. I wanted to see my grandparents. I also wanted to see Tokyo, where I was born.

My grandparents met us at the airport. We hugged and hugged. I felt so happy! They said I looked much bigger than before. I laughed. I look the same to me!

Greetings from
Tokyo

Then my grandparents took us to Tokyo. When I saw the city, I was surprised. There were so many cars and people and signs. I did not remember any of that!

Now we are back from Japan. I am happy because I have two countries to love—Japan and the United States.

Tell what happened to you. Tell how you felt about it.

Summary

In a **summary**, you tell about something you have read or seen. You write only the most important ideas. Read this article.

Corn Pops Up Everywhere!

What plant is used to make food, medicine, and fuel? What plant grows all over the world? The answer is corn!

Scientists think that thousands of years ago, native people of the Americas grew a corn plant that was good to eat. Explorers took the plant back to Europe. Corn farming spread quickly around the world after that.

One reason corn became so popular is that it grows well almost anywhere. It can grow in the mountains or by the sea. It can grow in rainy places and in dry places.

Corn is an important food. People eat cornbread, popcorn, and corn tortillas. Animals eat a lot of corn, too! Most of the corn grown in the U.S. is for cows, pigs, and other farm animals.

Corn is also used to make products such as glue, ink, and some medicines. There is even a fuel for cars made from corn. It helps gasoline burn better so there is less pollution.

Corn is very helpful!

Follow these steps to write a summary of the article:

1 Make a list of the most important ideas. These are the **main ideas**.

Corn is everywhere!
useful
has been around for thousands of years
grows almost anywhere
~~can grow in the mountains~~
A lot of food comes from corn.
~~Pigs eat corn.~~
used for other things besides food

2 Read through your list. Cross out details. Keep only the main ideas.

3 Turn your notes into sentences. Use your own words.

People have been growing corn for thousands of years. It is very useful, and it can grow almost anywhere. A lot of food is made from corn. Corn is used to make other products, too. Corn is very important!

The Good Writer Guide

How to Collect Ideas

To be a good writer, you need ideas. You can collect ideas from many places.

- **Look! Listen!** Pay attention everywhere you go. Take notes about what you hear. Draw what you see.

- **Read!** Read books, magazines, and newspapers. Search the Internet. When you read:

  - list fun facts.

  - write down words you like.

  - draw your favorite characters.

  - write questions.

  - list topics that you want to learn more about.

- **Brainstorm!** Think about a subject. What do you already know about it? What ideas can you get from other people? You can make a web to collect ideas.

- **Save Your Ideas.** You may use them later.

You can write ideas in a **notebook**.

You can write ideas on cards. Put them in a **file box**.

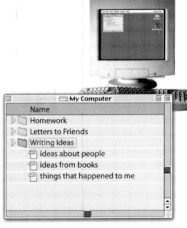

You can save ideas on a **computer**.

How to Write for a Purpose

Why are you writing? That is your reason, or **purpose**. There are many different purposes for writing.

1 You can **give information**. You can explain or tell facts about something. You can tell how to do something.

> ### The Saguaro
> The saguaro is a cactus plant that grows in hot, dry places. It has thick skin and prickly needles. Its long arms, or branches, reach up toward the sky.

2 You can **express yourself**. You can express your thoughts and feelings to other people. You can also write in a journal, just for you.

> February 1, 2003
>
> Today Aunt Camila is coming to visit. She is flying all the way from Costa Rica! I can't wait to see her.

3 You can **record ideas**. Write down things you want to remember. Tell what you think about something, such as a character in a story.

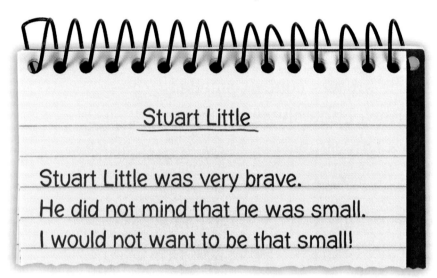

Stuart Little

Stuart Little was very brave.
He did not mind that he was small.
I would not want to be that small!

4 You can **invite someone**. You can ask the person to come to a special event. Tell the time and place of the event.

Come to a Birthday Party!

Where: Adam's house

When: Saturday, July 9,
at 12:00 p.m.

5 You can **describe**. You can tell what someone or something is like.

> ### The Old Barn
> Daria slowly opened the door to the old barn. It was dark inside. Only a little bit of light came in through a small window. The air was cold. It smelled like wet straw. Daria shivered. Suddenly, she heard a tiny squeak!

6 You can **write to learn**. Write things down to remember them better, to discover new things, and to develop new ideas.

What I learned from Sophie's report:

• Kinds of storms: hurricane, blizzard, typhoon

• A hurricane can have winds up to 160 miles per hour!

7 You can **entertain people**. You can write something that people will enjoy reading.

> Lunch
> My friend made me a sandwich.
> She started with some bread.
> She spread some jam,
> Then added ham.
> "YOU eat it," I said!

8 You can **thank someone**. Tell how much you like a gift you received or something that a person did.

> *July 14, 2003*
>
> Dear Ramesh,
>   Thank you for coming to my party. I like the baseball cap you gave me. The Padres are my favorite team! I will wear the cap all the time.
>
>   See you soon!
>   Adam

Choose a Form for Your Purpose

Once you know your purpose for writing, choose a writing form. For example:

■ If you want to **give information,** you could write:

How Tadpoles Become Frogs

Tadpoles hatch from eggs. In a few months, the tadpoles grow into adult frogs.

a report

Dear Hakeem,

Guess what! I found out that tadpoles can turn into frogs in two or three months!

a letter

■ If you want to **describe something** you could write:

Dear Jesse,

My new baby sister is so cute! Her skin is really soft.

a letter

My baby sister has Soft, dark skin, And a little dimple On her chin.

a poem

■ If you want to **entertain people**, you could write:

Jack: Mom! I sold the cow and got these magic beans!
Jack's mom (*very angry*): BEANS? You got BEANS?

a play script

Jack climbed the stalk
that grew from the beans.
He climbed and climbed,
Till he ripped his jeans!

a poem

■ If you want to **express yourself**, you could write:

Friday, August 7

I'm so happy. Dad says I can keep the stray kitten! I think I will name her Lucky because that's how I felt when I found her.

a journal entry

Lucky
When I got home from school yesterday, I found a surprise on the doorstep. It was a tiny kitten. She looked hungry and scared.

a story about you

How to Write for Your Audience

The people who read what you write are your **audience**. When you write, think about what your audience needs to know. Write in a way that fits your audience.

■ For **adults or people you don't know**, use formal language. Include **details** your audience may not know.

> My classmates and I have swimming lessons every Tuesday. We go to the pool at the YMCA. Our last swimming lesson was the best. We learned how to swim underwater.

■ For **your family**, write the way you talk. Leave out details your family already knows.

> Swimming was great! I can swim underwater now. I'll tell you all about it at dinner.

■ For **your friends**, write the way you talk to them. Use informal words. Tell about things that will interest your friends.

> My swimming lesson was awesome! I finally learned how to swim underwater. Paolo and Elizabeth were there, too. They are the best swimmers!

■ For **younger children**, use simple words that children will know. You may want to draw a picture, too.

> My swimming lesson was fun! Now I can swim underwater. My friends helped me.

How to Choose Words

Good writers read their writing many times. Each time, they work on it to make it better. Try these ways to make your writing sparkle!

Use Precise Words

Words that are **precise** make your writing clearer. They tell exactly what you mean. Use precise words to name people, places, and things.

Just OK

> She got her things. She put them in a bag. Then she looked around the room.

Much better!

> Tran got her jacket and soccer ball. She put them in a bag. Then she looked around her bedroom.

The writer used precise words to tell exactly **who**, **what**, and **where**.

Use Vivid Words

Vivid means "colorful" or "full of feeling." Vivid words help readers see, hear, taste, feel, or smell what is happening.

Just OK

Tran got her jacket and soccer ball. She put them in a bag. Then she looked around her bedroom.

Much better!

Tran grabbed her fuzzy, red jacket and soccer ball. She stuffed them in a big bag. Then she looked around her messy bedroom.

The writer used vivid words to give a clear picture.

You can use a special book, called a **thesaurus**, to find precise and vivid words.

How to Use a Thesaurus

A **thesaurus** is a special kind of book. It lists synonyms and antonyms for words.

■ **Synonyms** mean almost the same thing.

    little, small

■ **Antonyms** mean the opposite.

    little, big

Writers often use a thesaurus to find a vivid word.

To find a vivid word for **big**:

1. Look up the word **big** in the thesaurus. The words are listed in alphabetical order. Look at the **guide words** to help you find the page where **big** appears.

2. Look down the list of **entry words** until you see **big**. Find the synonyms.

> **big** The word **big** tells about the size of something.
>   **Synonyms** large, huge, enormous
>   **Antonyms** small, tiny, little

3. Choose the synonym that best describes what you want to say.

She stuffed them in a ~~big~~ huge bag.

This **guide word** matches the **first word** on the **left page**.

This **guide word** matches the **last word** on the **right page**.

baby

entry word

big

baby A **baby** is a very young child or animal.
   Synonyms infant, child
   Antonyms adult, grown-up

bad Something that is **bad** is something you do not like. It can also be something you should not do.
   Synonyms awful, horrible, terrible
   Antonyms good, great

beat When you **beat** a drum, you hit it to make a sound.
   Synonyms hit, pound, strike

28

beautiful Something that looks or sounds very nice is **beautiful**.
   Synonyms pretty, lovely
   Antonym ugly

below **Below** means to be lower than something else.
   Synonyms beneath, under
   Antonyms above, over

big The word **big** tells about the size of something.
   Synonyms large, huge, enormous
   Antonyms small, tiny, little

The elephant is **big**.

29

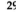

The Good Writer THESAURUS

How to Write Better Sentences

Write Complete Sentences

A sentence begins with a **capital letter**. It has an **end mark**.

Examples: The soccer game is today.
What time does the game begin?
We do not want to be late!

A sentence tells a complete thought.

Not OK

> Her mother.

OK

> Her mother waited downstairs.

Not OK

> ran out of her room

OK

> Tran ran out of her room.

Combine Short Sentences

Too many short sentences can sound choppy.
Combine them into longer sentences.

Just OK

> Tran ran out of her room.
> Tran ran down the stairs.

Better

> Tran ran out of her room
> and down the stairs.

You can use the word **and** to join two sentences.

Just OK

> Tran forgot the bag. Tran ran upstairs to get it.

Better

> Tran forgot the bag and ran upstairs to get it.

Fix Run-on Sentences

A **run-on** sentence uses the word **and** too many times. Turn a run-on sentence into two sentences.

Not OK

> Tran forgot the bag upstairs and she ran up the stairs to get it and she raced back down the stairs.

OK

> Tran forgot the bag and ran upstairs to get it. Then she raced back down the stairs.

or

> Tran forgot the bag upstairs. She ran up the stairs to get it and then raced back down the stairs.

Use Different Kinds of Sentences

When you write, include **statements, questions,** and **exclamations**. A good mix makes your writing more interesting.

Tran grabbed her fuzzy, red jacket and soccer ball. She stuffed them in a huge bag. Then she looked around her messy bedroom. Her mother waited downstairs. Tran ran out of her room and down the stairs. ~~Tran forgot the~~

Oh no! Where was the bag? It was still in her room! Tran ~~bag and~~ ran upstairs to get it. Then she raced back down the stairs.

How to Add Details

Details make your writing more interesting. You can add details to tell **what**, **when**, **where**, and **how**.

Just OK

> Tran loved to play soccer. She wanted to be on a soccer team. Tran practiced a lot. Soon she was good.

Much better!

> Tran loved to play soccer. She wanted to be on the school soccer team. Every day Tran went to the park and practiced. Soon she was good enough to join the team.

Show, Don't Tell

Use **actions** to show how a character feels or thinks. Use **dialogue**, or a person's words, to show what the character is like.

This tells

> The game was close. Tran felt nervous and excited. She wanted the coach to put her in the game. Tran was ready to play.

This shows

> The score was tied. There was only one minute left. Tran couldn't stand still.
> "Please give me a chance, Coach!" Tran begged. "I know I can do it!"
> "Yes, I think you're ready. You've scored a lot of goals in practice," he answered.

Tran's actions show that she is nervous and excited. Tran's words, or dialogue , show that she tries hard and does not give up.

Review Your Writing

■ **Save** your writing in a **portfolio** so you can review it often. A portfolio is a place to save special papers.

folder file   **big envelopes**   **notebook**

■ **Sort** your writing in groups that make sense to you.

Put your writing in the order that it was written.

Or, keep the same kinds of writing together.

■ **Think about your writing.** Read the writing in your portfolio. Think about what you did well. Set goals for how you can make your writing better. Ask yourself:

✓ What is my best piece of writing? Why?

✓ How has my writing changed?

✓ What can I do to make my writing better?

✓ What other kinds of writing do I want to try?

I like my story about the soccer game. It has a funny ending.

I want to write funny poems.

I will learn to use a thesaurus. Then my words will be more vivid.

Chapter 4
Present It!

Life in El Salvador

You have something important to say! Learn how to present ideas when you speak and write. Then people will get the idea!

Read Aloud

One way to **present**, or share, a story is to read it out loud to others.

Read-Aloud Tips

✔ Read loudly and clearly enough for everyone to hear.

✔ Make your voice sound like what is happening in the story.

✔ Stop for a moment after a very exciting or important part.

✔ Show the pictures.

Listen to a Story

When you listen to someone read a book, listen to understand and enjoy the story.

Listening Tips

✔ Make a picture of the story in your mind.

✔ Look at the pictures in the book.

✔ Pay attention to the reader's voice and face.

✔ Remember to have fun!

"The wolf tumbled down, down, and bumped his head."

Give a Message

A **message** is information that one person gives to another person. When you give a message, you give information that the person needs to know.

Speaking Tips

✔ Get your listeners' attention.

✔ Make your message as simple as possible.

✔ Check to see if your message is understood.

✔ Repeat your message if necessary.

The library closes in five minutes.

Get a Message

When you get a message, listen carefully.
Show that you understand the message.

Okay, I understand.

I do not understand.

That's great!

I am surprised!

Give a Talk

To tell information about a topic,
you can give a talk.

Speaking Tips

✔ Think about what you will say. Make **notes**.

✔ Think about who will listen to your talk.
They are your **audience**.

Your Audience	How to Speak to Them
Friends	Talk as you usually do.
Younger children	Use easier words.
Parents and teachers	Use formal language.

✔ Practice your talk.

✔ Make charts and pictures.

✔ Show the real things if you can.
These are called **props**.

✔ Look at your audience.

notes

prop

speaker

Listen to a Talk

When you are in the **audience**, listen to get information.

VEHICLES

FIRETRUCK

Listening Tips

✓ Look at the speaker.

✓ Sit quietly.

✓ Listen carefully.

✓ Look at charts and pictures.

✓ Pay attention to details.

✓ Raise your hand to ask a question.

audience

Talk in a Group

When you have a **discussion**, you talk in a group. People in the group take turns speaking and listening.

Speaking Tips

✓ Talk only about the topic.

✓ Ask questions.

✓ Take turns.

✓ If you do not know how to say something one way, try another way.

I like the story. It's funny. I laughed at the end.

Listen in a Group

When you are part of a discussion, listen to learn what others think.

Listening Tips

✔ Look at the speaker.

✔ Listen carefully.

✔ Wait to speak or to ask questions.

✔ Think about the speaker's ideas. Are they the same as your ideas?

I think the story is funny, too!

Find and Make Pictures

Pictures can help you tell about ideas and information.

Where to Find Pictures

Cut pictures from old magazines and newspapers.

Print pictures from the Internet.

Look for pictures in books.

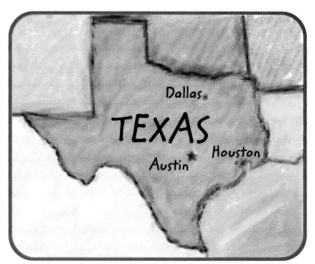

Create your own diagrams, graphs, and maps.

Present It!

When to Use Pictures

Use pictures for reports, announcements, and talks.

photograph

map

graph

Tips for Using Pictures

✓ Use photographs to show how something real looks.

✓ Draw pictures to show details.

✓ Use diagrams, graphs, and maps to help explain things.

View Pictures

When you look at pictures, think about **why** you are looking at them.

Look at pictures to **understand** more about something.

Look at pictures to **learn how** to make or do something.

Look at pictures to **have fun!**

My dog is so cute!

Present It!

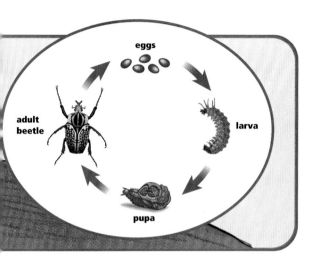

eggs

adult beetle

larva

pupa

Viewing Tips

✓ Look at details in photographs. Notice color, shape, and size.

The legs are long. There are six.

The body is black and yellow.

✓ When you look at diagrams, see how parts work together.

A B

The ends go together here.

✓ When you look at maps, notice where things are.

Baker Street

PET STORE

Maple Street

Here is the pet store.

Handwriting and Spelling Guide

Make sure your audience can read your work. Use your best handwriting, or **penmanship**, and spell each word correctly.

Hold your pencil this way.

Sit up straight.

Put both feet on the floor.

Get Ready to Write

Good handwriting starts with how you sit at your desk and hold your pencil.

If you are left-handed:

If you are right-handed:

Manuscript Alphabet

Capital Letters

A B C D E
F G H I J K
L M N O P
Q R S T U
V W X Y Z

Lowercase Letters and Numbers

a b c d e f g h
i j k l m n o p q
r s t u v w x y z
1 2 3 4 5 6 7 8 9 10

Write Letters

■ Make letters the **right size**.

Not OK	Not OK	OK

too big

too small

■ Make letters the **right shape**.

Not OK	Not OK	OK

■ Put the **right amount of space** between the letters in a word.

Not OK	Not OK	OK

too far

too close

Write Words and Sentences

- Start each sentence with a capital letter.
- End each sentence with an end mark.

Not OK

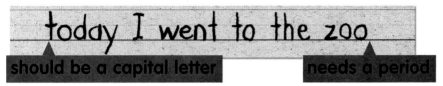

today I went to the zoo

should be a capital letter   needs a period

OK

Today I went to the zoo.

- Put more space between words than between letters.
- Put the same amount of space between each word.

Not OK

I sawa sleepy   bear.

not enough space   too much space

OK

I saw a sleepy bear.

Write Sentences in a Paragraph

- **Indent**, or leave a space, at the beginning of each paragraph.

- Leave blank spaces, or **margins**, on the top, bottom, left, and right of your writing.

- Leave more space between sentences than between words.

Indent each paragraph.

Start your writing at the left **margin**.

Alligators are reptiles that live in marshes and swamps. They have tough skin, short legs, and long tails. Their large jaws have many sharp teeth.

Cursive Alphabet

Capital Letters

Lowercase Letters

Write Words

■ **Connect** the letters.

Not OK	Not OK	OK

■ Make letters the **right size and shape**.

Not OK	Not OK	OK

■ Do not put letters too far apart or too close together.

Not OK	Not OK	OK

too far too close

Write Sentences

■ Put a space between words.

Not OK

Earth goesaround thesun.

should be a space

OK

Earth goes around the sun.

■ Make sure your letters sit on the bottom line.

Not OK

Earth also spins.

should be on the bottom line

OK

Earth also spins.

Write Sentences in a Paragraph

- **Indent**, or leave a space, at the beginning of each paragraph.

- Leave blank spaces, or **margins**, on the top, bottom, left, and right of your writing.

- Leave more space between sentences than between words.

Not OK

> The Moon and the Earth
>
> The Moon is very different from the Earth. Unlike the Earth the Moon does not have air or water. Nothing lives on the Moon.

OK

The first sentence is **indented**.

The writing begins at the **left margin**.

The writing leaves space for the **right margin**.

The Moon and the Earth

The Moon is very different from the Earth. Unlike the Earth the Moon does not have air or water. Nothing lives on the Moon.

Spell Sounds in English

Say the word you want to spell.
Write the letters that spell the sounds.

Spell Consonant Sounds

b

<u>b</u>all

ca<u>b</u>

c

<u>c</u>at

d

<u>d</u>esk

re<u>d</u>

f

fish

leaf

cuff

g

gate

pig

egg

h

hand

j

jar

Spelling Tip

Some words end in **ff**, **gg**, **ll**, **ss**, or **zz**. You hear only one consonant sound at the end of these words, but remember to write the same consonant twice.

Spell Consonant Sounds, *continued*

k

key

beak

back

Spelling Tip

Key and **cat** begin with the same sound. Spell the sound with **k** when the letter **e** or **i** comes next.

Spelling Tip

If the vowel is short, like the **a** in **back**, you usually write **c** before **k**.

l

lamp

heel

bell

m

map

drum

n

net

can

sign

knife

Spelling Tip

Some words have a silent letter before **n**. Did you **kn**ow that?

p

pizza

cup

q

quilt

Spelling Tip

Always keep the letters **qu** together. They spell the first two sounds you hear in **quilt**.

Spell Consonant Sounds, *continued*

r

red

wrist

Spelling Tip

Some words have a silent **w** before **r**. Can you think of another word? Here's a clue:

wr

s

seed

ki**ss**

t

ten

ha**t**

mi**tt**

v

van

Spelling Tip

Words never end in **v**. Write **ve** at the end of words like **have** and **give**.

w

wagon

x

si**x**

y

yellow

z

zero

fi**zz**

Spell Short Vowel Sounds

short a

apple

man

short e

egg

jet

short i

inch

pin

short o

ox

pot

short U

up

bus

Spell One Sound with Two Letters

shell

fi**sh**

whale

thumb

ba**th**

ri**ng**

chin

pea**ch**

ma**tch**

Spelling Tip

If the vowel is short, like the **a** in **match**, you usually write **t** before **ch**.

Spell Two Sounds with Two Letters

gi**ft**

o**ld** be**lt**

la**mp**

ha**nd**

ba**nk**

a**nt**

di**sk**

ne**st**

truck

brush

green

frog

drum

crow

clock

plant

flag

smell

snap

stamp

Spell Long Vowels

long a

c**a**k**e**

s**ai**l

gr**ay**

long e

f**ee**t

s**ea**

bunn**y**

long i

k**i**t**e**

t**ie**

n**igh**t

sk**y**

long O

r**o**p**e**

cr**ow**

b**oa**t

t**oe**

long U

t**u**b**e**

bl**ue**

fr**ui**t

Spelling Tip

Some very short words end with a long vowel sound. Just write one letter for the long vowel sound in these words:

be	he	me	go	no
she	hi	we	so	

Spell Words with *c* and *g*

hard c

cat

cot

cup

soft c

city

cent

ri**ce**

hard g

gate

go

gum

soft g

ginger

gem

Spelling Tip

Use **ge** in words like **age** and **huge** that have a long vowel. Use **dge** in words like **bridge** and **edge** that have a short vowel.

Spell Words with Vowel + *r*

st**ar**

h**or**n

f**er**n

t**ur**n

b**ir**d

ch**air**

b**ear**

Spelling Tip

Say the word you want to spell. Listen for the **r**. Does **r** come after the vowel like **bird**, or before the vowel like **brick**?

t**ear**

d**eer**

Spell More Vowel Sounds

c**oi**n

b**oy**

Spelling Tip

The letters **oi** and **oy** spell the same sound. Use **oy** if you hear the sound at the end of a word.

cl**ou**d

cr**ow**n

Spelling Tip

The letters **ou** and **ow** spell the same sound. Use **ow** if you hear the sound at the end of a word like **now**.

m**oo**n

scr**ew**

l**au**nch

s**aw**

s**al**t

b**all**

Spelling Tip

If you can spell **ball**, you can spell **call**, **fall**, **tall**, **small**, and **wall**.

b**oo**k

Spelling Tip

If you can spell **book**, you can spell **brook**, **cook**, **hook**, **look**, and **took**.

Spell Words with *-ed*, *-ing*, *-er*, *-est*

■ Just add the ending to words like **lift** and **rain**.

Examples: lift + ed = lift**ed**   rain + ing = rain**ing**

1 vowel +
2 consonants

2 vowels +
1 consonant

■ When a word ends in silent **e**, drop the **e**.
Then add the ending.

Examples: hop~~e~~ + ed = hop**ed**

rid~~e~~ + ing = rid**ing**

nic~~e~~ + er = nic**er**

nic~~e~~ + est = nic**est**

larg**e**

larg **er**

- When a word ends in one vowel and one consonant, double the consonant. Then add the ending.

  Examples: hop + p + ed = hopp**ed**

  skip + p + ing = skipp**ing**

  big + g + er = bigg**er**

  big + g + est = bigg**est**

- When a word ends in a consonant and **y**, change **y** to **i**. Then add -**ed**, -**er**, or -**est**.

  Examples: study + ed = studi**ed**

  happy + er = happi**er**

  happy + est = happi**est**

- Keep the **y** when you add -**ing**

  Examples: fly + ing = fly**ing**

  try + ing = try**ing**

  study + ing = study**ing**

Spell Plurals

■ Add -**s** to most words.

Examples:

pot + s = pot**s**   kite + s = kite**s**

■ Add -**es** to words that end in **s**, **ch**, **sh**, **x**, or **z**.

Examples:

glass + es = glass**es**   peach + es = peach**es**

brush + es = brush**es**   box + es = box**es**

■ Change **y** to **i** . Add -**es**.

Examples:

baby + es = babi**es**   puppy + es = puppi**es**

Spell Long Words

■ Say the word and count the parts. Spell each part. Then read the word.

   Example: bas + ket = basket

The word is **basket**. I hear two parts. I'll write the first part: **bas**. Then I'll write the second part: **ket**.

■ Is the long word made up of two smaller words? Write each word.

   Example: week + end = weekend

■ Does the word have the first sound in **about**? Start with **a**.

   Examples: along   across   around   alone

■ Does the word end like **apple**? Many words end in a **consonant** + **le**.

   Examples: candle   little   table   title

> ### Spelling Tip
> If the word has a long vowel sound like **table** and **title**, write only one consonant before **le**.

Spell These Right!

Some words are hard to spell. You can look here to check your spelling.

Words That Sound Alike

its
it's

Its fur is dirty.

It's time for a bath.

Spelling Tip

Say the sentence. Does "it is" make sense? If so, use **it's**.

knew
new

She **knew** the answer.

She has a **new** pencil.

Spelling Tip

Think about the word's meaning. **New** means the opposite of **old**.

know
no

Do you **know** how to dance?

No, I can't dance.

our
hour

Our bus is late!

It will be here in one **hour**.

they're
there
their

They're playing on the swings.

There is a bee on **their** dad!

through
threw

She walked **through** the gate.

He **threw** her a ball.

two
to
too

Two friends are going **to** the movies.

Can we go, **too**?

wear
where

I want to **wear** my red jacket.

Where is it?

your
you're

Your book report is great!

You're learning to spell.

Spelling Tip

Say the sentence. Does "you are" make sense? If so, use **you're**.

Words That Kids Misspell

above
> The clock is **above** the door.

again
> Let's sing this song **again**.

almost
> I can **almost** reach the shelf.

always
> She **always** uses a blue pen.

another
> I need **another** piece of paper.

anyone
> Does **anyone** want more cake?

are
> You **are** in the wrong seat!

beautiful
> Your new dress is **beautiful**.

because
> He can't play **because** he is sick.

before
> I wash my hands **before** I eat.

could
> You **could** be an astronaut.

country
> Mexico is a **country**.

different
> We are on two **different** teams.

enough
> There is **enough** cake for ten.

especially
> I **especially** liked the panda.

everything
> **Everything** is ready for the party.

except
> I like all fruit, **except** for peaches.

excited
> She's **excited** about her new toy.

favorite
> Blue is my **favorite** color.

first
> This is the **first** time I tried to skate.

friends
> She likes to play with her **friends**.

getting
> He is **getting** good grades now.

into

They jumped **into** the pool.

laugh

I like to **laugh** at your jokes.

myself

I baked this bread by **myself**!

people

The city is full of **people**.

really

We **really** miss you!

said

They **said**, "Hi!"

school

I take the bus to **school**.

something

They forgot **something**.

sometimes

Sometimes Jill is late for school.

terrible

Last night there was a **terrible** storm.

thought

I **thought** I saw a bear!

trouble

We had **trouble** lifting the heavy boxes.

until

Wait **until** the light turns green.

usually

I **usually** study in my room.

very

You did a **very** good job!

want

Do you **want** an apple?

were

They **were** in the same class last year.

who

Who is your teacher?

Spelling Tips

Here are some tips to help you spell words correctly.

1. Look at the new word.

2. Look again and **say** the word.

3. Listen to the word as you **say it again**.

4. Make a picture of the word in your head.

5. Spell the word out loud several times.

6. Write the word five or ten times.

7. Check the word. Look in a dictionary.

8. Use the word in a sentence.

Use a Dictionary

Use a dictionary to find out the meaning or spelling of a word. All dictionaries list the words in **alphabetical order**, or from A to Z.

Picture Dictionary

A **picture dictionary** uses mainly pictures and examples to show the meaning of a word.

Look at the **first letter** of your word. To look up the word **idea**, turn to the page that shows the letter **i**.

The **second letter** of each word is in **alphabetical order**, too. The word **idea** comes after **ice** because **d** comes after **c**.

Examples and pictures help you understand what a word means.

alphabetical order

Ii

imagine
It is fun to **imagine** things.

ice
You can skate on **ice**.

ice
ice skate

include
The teacher will **include** everyone in the activity.

idea
What a good **idea**!

step stool

information
You can find **information** in many places.

book

ill
Geena is **ill** today.

computer

a b c d e f g h **i** j k l m n o p q r s t u v w x y z

47

Beginning Dictionary

A **beginning dictionary** uses simple words to explain the meaning of a word. Sometimes a beginning dictionary also gives examples and pictures.

These words are **guide words**. They show the first and last words on the page. Use the guide words to help you find your word.

fountain / fresh

Alexander was hot and thirsty and was happy to find this **fountain**.

fountain
A fountain is a stream of water that shoots up into the air. Some fountains are pretty to look at. Other fountains are used for drinking. ▲ **fountains**.

Fourth of July
The **Fourth of July** is an American holiday that celebrates the birthday of the United States. It is also called **Independence Day**.

fox
A **fox** is a wild animal. Most **foxes** look like small, thin dogs, but they have thick fur and a big tail. They also have large ears that are pointed and a long nose. ▲ **foxes**.

free
1. **Free** means that a person does not have to pay any money for something. The magic show in the park is **free**. There is a **free** toy in every box of that cereal.
2. **Free** also means not held back or kept in. The cat was **free** to walk around.
▲ **freer, freest**.

freeze
Freeze means to become solid when it is very cold. When water **freezes**, it changes into ice. We skated on the pond after it **froze**.
▲ **froze, frozen, freezing**.

fresh
1. When something is **fresh**, it has just been made, done, or gathered. We ate **fresh** tomatoes from June's garden. Our supermarket sells **fresh** fish. This bread was baked this morning and is very **fresh**.
2. **Fresh** also means not having salt. Water in rivers, lakes, and ponds is **fresh** water. Water in the ocean is salt water. ▲ **fresher, freshest**.

136

A **definition** uses simple words to explain the meaning of a word.

Sometimes a word has more than one meaning.

Examples help you understand what a word means and how to use it.

Chapter 5
Grammar Made Graphic

Marcus

puts it together.

Sometimes English is like a puzzle. How do you put the pieces together? You can learn the rules of grammar.

noun verb

Lisa helps Marcus.
↓
She helps Marcus.

period

pronoun

Sentences

A sentence is a complete thought.

Lydia

Lydia rides the bus.

rides the bus.

All sentences start with a **capital letter**.

    Example: **M**any people work in the city.

There are four kinds of sentences.

❶ Statements

A statement tells something. It ends with a **period**.

    Examples: People walk to their jobs.
                 A policeman stops the traffic. **period**

❷ Questions

A question asks for information. It ends with a **question mark**.

There are many ways to start a question.

Examples:

Are the hot dogs good?   **Which** balloons are for sale?

How much is a hot dog?   **Do** you want the big balloon?

Is there some mustard?   **Does** it have a string?

Where are the buns?   **Can** the big balloon fly high?

Who wants pickles?   **When** can I take it?

question mark

③ Exclamations

A sentence that shows strong feeling is called an **exclamation**. It ends with an **exclamation point**.

Examples: Wow, the buildings are so tall! ◄ **exclamation point**

That car is going too fast!

④ Commands

A **command** tells you to do something. Many commands end with a **period**. If a command shows strong feeling, it ends with an **exclamation point**.

Examples: Stop at the corner. **period**

Please look both ways before you cross the street.

Watch out for that car!

exclamation point

Go To ► Practice A on page 322.

Negative Sentences

A negative sentence uses a **negative word** like **not** or **never**.

Example: She is happy.   She is **not** happy.

In a negative sentence, the word **not** comes after **am**, **is**, or **are**.

Examples:

I **am** **not** a good swimmer.

The water **is** **not** warm.

I am afraid of the water, but the other kids **are** **not** afraid.

They **are** **never** tired of the water!

Use only one negative word in a sentence.

Our pool is ~~not~~ never closed.

Go To Practice B on page 322.

Complete Sentences

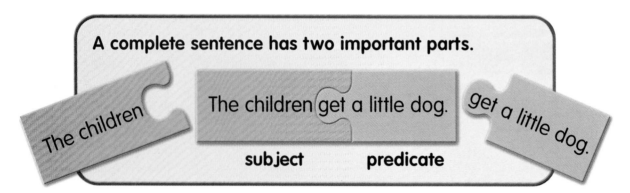

A complete sentence has two important parts.

The children

The children get a little dog.

get a little dog.

subject   predicate

■ Every sentence has two parts.

The **subject** tells whom or what the sentence is about.

Mom is tired.

She sits on the bench.

The children play with their dog.

The brown dog has a stick.

The stick is long.

The **predicate** tells what the subject is, does, or has.

Go To ▶ Practices C and D on page 323.

Longer Sentences

> You can use **and** or **or** to combine two short sentences into a longer sentence.
>
> **Example:** Juan goes to the pool.
> Tina goes to the pool.
> Juan **and** Tina go to the pool.

■ You can combine the **subjects** of two sentences.

Examples:

1. **Juan** likes the pool.
   Tina likes the pool.
   Juan and Tina like the pool.

2. **Juan's dad** takes them.
   Tina's mom takes them.
   Juan's dad or Tina's mom takes them.

■ You can combine the **predicates** of two sentences.

Examples:

3. Juan **likes to dive**.
   Juan **likes to splash**.
   Juan **likes to dive and splash**.

4. Tina **swims**.
   Tina **goes down the slide**.
   Tina **swims or goes down the slide**.

Longer Sentences, continued

■ You can also combine two sentences into a compound sentence. Use **and**, **but**, or **or**.

and	Use **and** to put together two ideas that are alike. Tina went to the pool. + Then she went shopping. Tina went to the pool**,** **and** then she went shopping.
but	Use **but** to put together two ideas that show a difference. Juan had fun on the slide. + He did not like the diving board. Juan had fun on the slide**,** **but** he did not like the diving board.
or	Use **or** to show a choice between two ideas. Tina can swim after school. + She can do her homework. Tina can swim after school**,** **or** she can do her homework.

Grammar Tip

When you connect two sentences with **and**, **but**, or **or**, you make a **compound sentence**. You use a `comma` in a compound sentence.

Go To ▶ Practices E and F on page 324.

Write Sentences

When you write, use different kinds of sentences. They make your writing interesting.

Example: Pam looks up at the building. How tall is it? Wow! The top reaches the clouds!

Pam looks at the wide city street.

It is full of cars and buses. The traffic

What is wrong? Oh, now she can see!

does not move. ∧Too many people are

and

crossing the street. Many cars ~~honk~~

~~their horns.~~ ~~Many~~ trucks honk

They are loud!

their horns. ∧

The writer added different kinds of sentences, and she combined two sentences at the end. Now the writing is more interesting.

Common Nouns

Some words name people, animals, places, or things. These naming words are called **nouns**.

Examples:

Person	Animal	Place	Thing
girl	dog	park	bench

The **girl** takes her **dog** to the **park**. They sit on a **bench**.

■ Some **nouns** name **people** or **animals**.

Examples: The **girl** and her **mother** feed a **duck**.
The **dog** chases a **bird**.

Can you name other **people** and **animals** in the picture?

Grammar Made Graphic

■ Some **nouns** name **things**.

Examples: When it's time to eat, they find a **table**.
It is near a pretty **flower**.
The girl and her mom eat a **sandwich**.
The dog eats out of his **bowl**.

Can you name other **things** in the picture?

Common Nouns, continued

■ Some **nouns** name **places**.

> **Examples:** The girl and her mom leave the **park**.
> They walk along the **street**.
> They pass by the **museum**.
> They stop and look in a **store**.

Can you name other **places** in the picture?

Grammar Made Graphic

Proper Nouns

A **proper noun** is the name of a special person, animal, place, or thing. Start a proper noun with a capital letter.

Example:

I see a boy with a cat.

Oh, it's **Bill** with his cat **Fluffy**!

Which nouns name special people and animals?

People and Animals	
girl	Lynn
boy	Bill
cat	Fluffy

Which nouns name special places?

Places	
store	Books and More
street	West Street
park	Chávez Park

Which nouns start with a capital letter?

Go To ▶ Practice A on page 325.

More than One

A **singular noun** names one person, animal, place, or thing. A **plural noun** names more than one.

Example: You can buy one **book** or many **books** at the store.

■ Add **-s** to most nouns to show more than one.

One	More than One
cat	cat**s**
kite	kite**s**
flower	flower**s**

■ Add **-es** to nouns that end in **s**, **ss**, **x**, **ch**, **sh**, and **z**.

One	More than One
glass	glass**es**
box	box**es**
lunch	lunch**es**
dish	dish**es**

Grammar Made Graphic

■ For nouns that end in **-y**, change the **y** to <u>**i**</u> and then add **-<u>es</u>**.

One	More than One
cherry	cherr**<u>ies</u>**
berry	berr**<u>ies</u>**
baby	bab**<u>ies</u>**

■ A few nouns change in special ways to show more than one.

One	More than One
man	men
woman	women
child	children
foot	feet

Go To ▶ Practice B on page 325.

Grammar Made Graphic

A, An, and The

> **The words <u>a</u>, <u>an</u>, and <u>the</u> often come just before a noun.**
>
> **Example:** You can get **<u>a</u> hat** and **<u>an</u> apple** at **<u>the</u> carnival**.

■ Use **<u>a</u>** or **<u>an</u>** when you are not thinking of something specific.

Examples: Efram plans to go to **<u>an</u> event** this year.

He wants to play **<u>a</u> game**.

He wants to get **<u>a</u> bag** of popcorn.

CITY EVENTS

May 7   Spring Carnival at Adams School

July 4   Fourth of July Picnic in Chávez Park

October 7   Fall Festival at Central Square

December 12   Winter Wonderland at Harding Mall

■ Use **<u>a</u>** if the next word starts with a **consonant**.

Examples: **<u>a</u> f**estival

<u>a</u> carnival

<u>a</u> game

■ Use **<u>an</u>** if the next word starts with a **vowel or silent h**.

Examples: **<u>an</u> a**nimal

<u>an</u> event

<u>an</u> idea

<u>an</u> orchestra

<u>an</u> umbrella

<u>an</u> hour

■ Use **<u>the</u>** when you are thinking of something specific.

Examples: Efram goes to **<u>the</u> Spring Carnival**.
He watches **<u>the</u> puppets**.
He likes **<u>the</u> popcorn** that his father bought.

Go To Practice C on page 326.

Possessive Nouns

A **possessive noun** is the name of an owner.
The name always has an apostrophe (').

Examples: **Mike's** trucks are very big.
The **trucks'** noise is very loud!

Study these examples to learn where to write the apostrophe.

■ For one owner, add the apostrophe **'** plus **s**.

■ For more than one owner, just add the apostrophe **'**.

One Owner	More than One Owner
the **car's** horn	the **cars'** horns
the **worker's** hammer	the **workers'** hammers

The **car's** horn wakes me up in the morning.

I know! The **trucks'** engines are really loud, too!

Go To ▶ Practice D on page 326.

Use Nouns in Writing

Use **precise nouns** to help your reader know just what you are writing about.

Example: A **car** parks outside the **office**.
A **taxi** parks outside the **clinic**.

City Noises

I do not need an alarm. The

city noises wake me up. I hear

the ~~sound~~ toot of a taxi rushing along

the street. I hear the ~~noise~~ clang and bang of trash

cans in the alley. I hear the wail

of ~~a car~~ an ambulance. Toot, clang, wail! It is

time to get up!

The writer changed the words **sound** and **noise** to be specific.

The word **car** is good, but **ambulance** is even more precise!

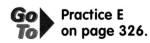 **Practice E** on page 326.

Pronouns

> A **pronoun** can take the place of a noun.
>
> Example: **Clare** writes a letter.
>
> **She** writes a letter.

You can use these pronouns in the subject of a sentence. Be sure to use the pronoun that tells about the right number of people.

■ Use **I** for yourself.

■ Use **we** for yourself and another person.

One	More than One
I	we
you	you
he, she, it	they

I finished my letter.

We will take it to the post office.

I want to go, too. Can **we** take Boomer?

Grammar Tip

Always capitalize the pronoun **I**, wherever it appears in a sentence.

■ Use **you** when you talk to one person or to more than one person.

Pronouns, continued

■ When you talk about one other person:

- Use **he** for a boy or a man.

- Use **she** for a girl or a woman.

Grammar Made Graphic

When you talk about more than one person, use **they**.

Pronouns, continued

■ When you talk about places and things:

- Use **it** for one place or thing.
- Use **they** for more than one place or thing.

We will send a gift to the kids. **It** will be a big surprise!

We will buy paints and paper. **They** are good gifts.

Try these markers, too. **They** make bright colors.

Go To Practice A on page 327.

> **Some pronouns tell who owns something.**
>
> **Example:** This is **Clare's** letter.
>
> This is **her** letter.

■ Use the pronoun that tells about the right person or people.

One	More than One
my — This is from **my** aunt and uncle.	**our** — I want to open **our** gift.
your — **Your** paintbrush is the black one.	**your** — May I have some of **your** paper?
his, her, its	**their**
Ray is still using **his** brush. Clare finishes **her** picture. She puts the marker back in **its** place.	Ray and Dad are still working on **their** pictures!

Go To ▶ Practice B on page 328.

Pronouns, continued

Remember: A **pronoun** can take the place of a noun.

Examples: Mrs. Ramos needs **posters**.

Mrs. Ramos needs **them**.

Clare will make some for **Mrs. Ramos**.

Clare will make some for **her**.

■ Use these pronouns after action verbs or after words like **to**, **for**, **at**, **of**, or **with**.

One	More than One
me	us
you	you
him, her, it	them

- Use **me** for yourself.

- Use **us** for yourself and another person.

- Use **you** to talk to other people.

Grammar Made Graphic

- Use **him** for one boy or one man.
- Use **her** for one girl or one woman.
- Use **it** for one place or thing.
- Use **them** for more than one person, place, or thing.

Give this marker to **him**. They can use **it** to make the posters.

Clare will make the posters. I will help **her**.

When you finish the posters, I will hang **them** in the neighborhood.

Go To Practice C on page 328.

Grammar Made Graphic

This, That, These, Those

Will you plant **these** flowers?

We need to paint **this** bench.

Please trim **those** bushes.

Rake under **that** tree.

Go To   Practice D on page 329.

Use Pronouns in Writing

When you repeat the same noun too often, your writing is not very interesting. Change some nouns to pronouns. Make sure you use the correct pronoun!

Example: My friend and I picked up trash at the park.

~~My friend and I~~ We put ~~the trash~~ it in plastic bags.

The use of pronouns makes the paragraph sound better.

Neighborhood Clean-Up

Neighbors cleaned up the park on Saturday. Mr. Carter painted a bench. ~~Mr. Carter~~ He did a good job! ~~Mr. Carter's~~ His children, Ray and Clare, picked up leaves. ~~Ray and Clare~~ They filled up two bags.

Why did the writer change **his** to **her**?

Mrs. Sánchez and ~~his~~ her son worked hard, too. Their job was to plant flowers. Mr. and Mrs. Ross trimmed the bushes.

The park looks great now!

Go To Practice E on page 329.

Adjectives

> An **adjective** describes, or tells about, a <u>noun</u>.
>
> **Example:** The <u>car</u> went up a <u>hill</u>.
>
> The **red** <u>car</u> went up a **little** <u>hill</u>.

■ Many adjectives tell how something looks.
They tell about **size**, **color**, and **shape**.
How does this bus look?

size
The **big** bus takes
children to school.

color
The **yellow** bus
has **red** lights.

shape
The wheels on
the bus are **round**.

Go To ▶ Practice A on page 330.

■ Some adjectives tell "how many" or "how much".

Use **number words** to tell exactly how many things there are.

Examples: The train has **six** cars.
It has **one** engine.
The train will travel **120** miles to Houston.

Sometimes, you do not know the exact number. Then use the words in the chart.

More Ways to Tell "How Many" or "How Much"	
Use these words when it is possible to count things.	Use these words when it is not possible to count things.
a lot of cars **many** cars **several** cars	**much** rain **a lot of** rain
some cars **a few** cars	**a little** rain **some** rain **not much** rain **only a little** rain

Go To ▶ **Practice B** on page 330.

Adjectives That Compare

Adjectives can help you compare things.

"Compare" means to show how things are alike or different.

Example: This is a small car.
This car is smaller than that one.
This is the smallest car of all.

small
smaller
smallest

■ Add **-er** to an adjective to compare two things.
You will probably use the word **than** in your sentence, too.

Examples: The van is taller **than** the car.
The truck is cleaner **than** the van.

■ Add **-est** to an adjective to compare three or more things.
Use the word **the** before the adjective.

Examples: The truck is **the tallest** of the three.
The car is **the cleanest** of all.

Go To Practice C on page 331.

■ Do not add **-er** or **-est** to a long adjective.
Adjectives with three or more syllables would be
hard to say with **-er** or **-est** at the end.
Use **more** or **most** with long adjectives.

Examples:

The blue car is expensive.
The black van is more expensive than the blue car.
The red car is **the most expensive** car of all.

■ Some adjectives have special forms for comparing things.

bad	**worse**	**worst**
This taxi looks **bad**.	This taxi looks **worse**.	This taxi looks the **worst** of all!

good	**better**	**best**
This bus looks **good**.	This bus looks **better**.	This bus looks the **best** of all!

Go To Practice D on page 332.

Grammar Made Graphic

Adjectives in Sentences

You can use **adjectives** in the subject or predicate of a sentence.

Examples:

The **green** car | stops here.
subject | predicate

Its seats | are **green**, too.
subject | predicate

■ Most adjectives come before the nouns they tell about.

   Examples: The **green** car is on a **wide** street.

   The **little** truck has a **loud** motor.

■ An adjective can come after words like **is**, **are**, **look**, **feel**, **smell**, and **taste**. The adjective tells about the noun in the subject.

   Examples: Dad is **careful**.

   Kazuo feels **safe**.

Grammar Made Graphic

Use Adjectives in Writing

When you write, use adjectives. They help your reader see what you are writing about.

Example: The plane left the airport.
The silver plane left the huge airport.

My Trip on an Airplane

I went on a big, silver plane. It flew high in the sky. I saw two houses and many roads below. There were tiny cows and horses, too. Then we went up even higher. I saw fluffy clouds. They looked like white pillows, and I fell asleep. When we landed with a bump, I woke up. It was a great trip!

Now you know how many houses and roads the writer saw.

This **adjective** helps you picture the clouds.

Go To Practice E on page 332.

Action Verbs

An **action verb** tells what someone or something does.

Example: I **kick** the ball.

shout

wave

sit

jump

kick

Grammar Made Graphic

cheer

drink

stand

run

bark

269

The Verbs *Am, Is,* and *Are*

> Some verbs do not show action. These **verbs** tell what the subject of a sentence is or is like.
>
> Examples: Mr. Silva **is** the coach.
> He **is** happy.

■ Be sure to use the verb that goes with the subject.

1. Use **am** with **I**.   **2.** Use **is** with **he**, **she**, or **it**.

Hi! **I am** Mr. Silva.

He is the best coach!

3. Use **are** with **you**, **we**, or **they**.

Are they on Coach Silva's team, too?

Yes, **they are**.

We are all on Coach Silva's team! **Are you** on a team?

Go To ▶ Practice A on page 333.

The Verbs *Has* and *Have*

> **Some verbs tell what the subject of a sentence has.**
>
> **Examples:** This team **has** good players.
> We **have** a difficult game.

■ Be sure to use the verb that goes with the subject.

1. Use **have** with **I**   **2.** Use **has** with **he, she,** or **it**.

> **I have** a good
> idea for a play!

> **He** always **has**
> good ideas!

3. Use **have** with **you, we,** or **they**.

> **We have** the ball.
> **You have** a chance
> to score.

> Oh, no!
> **They have** a
> great goalie!

Go To Practice B on page 333.

Grammar Made Graphic

Actions in the Present

> **All action verbs show when the action happens.**
>
> Example: I **kick** the ball.
>
> This **verb** is in the **present tense**.
> The action is happening **now**.

■ Use **s** at the end of an action verb if the subject is **he**, **she**, or **it**.

He	The player **kicks** the ball. Tim **kicks** the ball. He **kicks** the ball.
She	The girl **kicks** the ball. Maritza **kicks** the ball. She **kicks** the ball.
It	The ball **rolls** into the goal. It **rolls** into the goal.

■ Do not use **s** for **I**, **you**, **we**, or **they**.

Examples: I **kick** the ball.
We **kick** the ball.
You **kick** the ball.
They **kick** the ball.

Go To ▶ Practices C and D on pages 334–335

Actions in the Past

You can add -<u>ed</u> to many action verbs to show that the action happened in the past.

Example: I **kicked** the ball.

This **verb** is in the **past tense**.

Compare the verbs in the chart.

	Now	In the Past
1.	We **play** a good game.	We **play<u>ed</u>** a good game yesterday.
2.	My friends **pass** me the ball.	My friends **pass<u>ed</u>** me the ball.
3.	I **kick** a goal!	I **kick<u>ed</u>** a goal!
4.	I **yell**, "GOAL!"	I **yell<u>ed</u>**, "GOAL!"
5.	My friends **cheer** for me.	My friends **cheer<u>ed</u>** for me.
6.	My mom and dad **kiss** me!	My mom and dad **kiss<u>ed</u>** me!

Go To Practices E and F on page 336.

More Actions in the Past

Some action verbs have special forms for the **past tense**.

Example:

Now	In the Past	
go	**went**	I **went** to the pool yesterday.

Compare the verbs in the chart.

	Now	In the Past
1.	I **bring** my friend Tina to the pool.	I **brought** my friend Tina to the pool.
2.	We **do** some stretches.	We **did** some stretches.
3.	We **get** ready to swim.	We **got** ready to swim.
4.	We **go** in the water.	We **went** in the water.
5.	I **give** Tina a lesson.	I **gave** Tina a lesson.
6.	She **holds** her breath.	She **held** her breath.
7.	She **makes** it across the pool.	She **made** it across the pool.
8.	Her mom **sees** her on the other side.	Her mom **saw** her on the other side.
9.	"Good job, Tina," she **says**.	"Good job, Tina," she **said**.
10.	Tina **takes** another swim, and I **take** a rest!	Tina **took** another swim, and I **took** a rest!

Go To ▶ Practice G on page 337.

> The verbs **was** and **were** tell about something that happened **in the past**.
>
> **Examples:**
>
> | Now | In the Past | |
> |-----|-------------|--|
> | am | **was** | I **was** a good teacher. |
> | are | **were** | Tina and I **were** in a race. |

Study this chart.

Now	In the Past
I **am**	I **was**
you **are**	you **were**
he, she, it **is**	he, she, it **was**
we **are**	we **were**
they **are**	they **were**

■ Use **was** and **were** to tell about the past.

• Use **was** with **I**.

   Example: I **was** very surprised.

• Use **was** with **he**, **she**, or **it**.

   Example: She **was** very fast!

• Use **were** with **you**, **we**, or **they**.

   Example: We won the race.
   We **were** so happy!

Practice H on page 338.

Actions in the Future

Some verbs tell what will happen later.

Example: I **will visit** you next winter.

I **am going to play** in the snow.

These **verbs** are in the **future tense**.

■ There are two ways to make a verb tell about the future.

• You can add **will** before the verb.

• You can write **am going to**, **are going to**, or **is going to** before the verb.

Next winter, we **will have** snow.

We **are going to make** a snowman.

María **is going to ride** on her sled.

Ahmed **will skate**.

■ In a negative sentence, put **not** just after **will**, **am**, **is**, or **are**.

Kim **will <u>not</u> sit** here.

He **is <u>not</u> going to play** tennis!

I **am <u>not</u> going to run**.

Go To ▶ Practice I on page 338.

Helping Verbs

A **helping verb** works with another verb. The other verb is called the main verb.

Examples: We **are** **playing** basketball.
We **can** **play** well!

Together, the helping verb and the main verb tell about an action.

■ Some verbs tell about an action as it is happening.

- These verbs use **am**, **is**, or **are** as the **helping verb**.

- They use **-ing** at the end of the **main verb**.

I **am** **running** fast.

He **is** **bouncing** the ball.

She **is** **reaching** for the ball.

They **are** **watching**.

■ Some **helping verbs** have special meanings.

- Use **can** to tell that someone is able to do an action.

  Example:

  I **can** **bounce** the ball!

- Use **may** and **might** to tell that something is possible.

  Examples:

  We **may** **play** again later.
  Our team **might** **win**.

- Use **must** and **should** to tell that somebody has to do something.

  Examples:

  We **must** **practice** more.
  I **should** **pass** the ball better.

Helping Verbs, continued

■ You can use a **helping verb** to start a question. The subject comes between the **helping verb** and the **main verb**.

> **Examples:** **Do** you **like** this game?
>
> **Does** Dad **play** this game?
>
> **Is** Mom **watching** us?
>
> **Are** they **looking** now?
>
> **Can** you **throw** the ball to me?

■ In a negative sentence, put <u>**not**</u> between the **helping verb** and the **main verb**.

Does he catch it?
No, he **does** <u>**not**</u> **catch** it.

Go To ▶ Practice J on page 339.

Use Verbs in Writing

Vivid verbs make your writing more interesting. They give your reader a good picture of the action.

Example: We **went** up to the ice and **skated** in.
We **rushed** up to the ice and **glided** in.

Can you see what the skater is doing? The **vivid verbs** help you see.

Ice Skating

Higher and higher
I **glide** in the sky,
My feet flashing silver,
A star in each eye.
With wind at my back
I can **float**, I can **soar**.
The earth cannot hold me
In place anymore.

—Sandra Liatsos

Go To Practice K on page 339.

Adverbs

An **adverb** can tell more about a **verb**.

Example: Josh **sleeps** in his room.
Josh **sleeps** **quietly** in his room.

■ Many adverbs tell **how** something happens.
These **adverbs** often end in **-ly**.

Examples: Josh **gets up** **quickly**.

Josh and Aunt Sue **walk** **fast** to the train station.

■ Some adverbs tell **where** something happens.

Examples: The subway **stops** **there**.

Josh and Aunt Sue **will travel** **north** on the train.

■ Some adverbs tell **when** something happens.

Examples: On Saturdays, they **always** **go** to the Science Center.

They **will arrive** **soon**.

Go To Practice A on page 340.

Use Adverbs in Writing

Use **adverbs** to tell where, when, and how things happen. These details help make your writing clear and interesting.

Example: Josh and Aunt Sue looked **carefully** at the exhibit in the Science Center.

Josh added adverbs to give important details.

The adverb **loudly** tells Grandma just how the dinosaur roared.

256 South Vista Drive
Silver City, Arizona
May 4, 2003

Dear Grandma,

Yesterday

I went with Aunt Sue to the Science Center. We go there every Saturday. There was a special dinosaur exhibit. Big robots showed how dinosaurs moved!

You can control the robots with levers, just like a video game. When you press a button, the dinosaurs roar loudly. It was a little scary. It was also very fun!

Love,
Josh

Practice B
on page 340.

Capital Letters

> A word that begins with a **capital letter** is special in some way.
>
> Example: **O**ur class will go to the **N**ational **A**irplane **M**useum.

■ Use a capital letter to show where a sentence begins.

Examples: **W**e will take an exciting trip next **M**onday!

Our class will visit a museum with all kinds of airplanes.

■ Always write the word **I** with a capital letter.

Who is coming?

You and **I** can make a list.

■ Use a capital letter for a person's
- **first name**
- **last name**
- initials
- title.

Class Trip List

Students	Parents
Billy **R**oss	**M**rs. Lane
Luisa Díaz	Ms. Kelly
J. **J**. Kelly	Dr. Díaz

Use these titles for people.
- **Mr.** for a man
- **Mrs.** for a married woman
- **Ms.** for any woman
- **Dr.** for a doctor

■ Begin the name of a day or a month with a capital letter. Also capitalize their abbreviations.

Days of the Week	
Sunday	Sun.
Monday	Mon.
Tuesday	Tues.
Wednesday	Wed.
Thursday	Thurs.
Friday	Fri.
Saturday	Sat.

Months of the Year	
January	Jan.
February	Feb.
March	Mar.
April	Apr.
May	
June	
July	
August	Aug.
September	Sept.
October	Oct.
November	Nov.
December	Dec.

These months are never abbreviated.

■ Begin each important word in the name of a special day or holiday with a capital letter.

Special Days and Holidays	
Christmas	Kwanzaa
Earth Day	Labor Day
Fourth of July	New Year's Day
Hanukkah	Thanksgiving

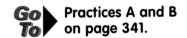

Go To ▶ Practices A and B on page 341.

Grammar Made Graphic

Capital Letters, continued

■ Use a capital letter for each important
word in the name of a special place.

Where is the National Airplane Museum?

It is on South Flight Street, in Silver City.

Names of Special Places		
Streets West Avenue First Street	**Continents** Africa Asia	**Public Places** Central Park Piney Woods
Cities and States Dallas, Texas Miami, Florida	**Bodies of Water** Pacific Ocean Red River	**Buildings** Washington Monument Empire State Building
Countries Chile United States	**Landforms** Rocky Mountains Great Plains	**Planets** Earth Mars

■ Sometimes special place names are shortened, or
abbreviated, but they still start with a capital letter.

Mom,
    Meet me at the Airplane Museum.
It's on 145 S. Flight St., near the corner
of Hwy. 101 N. and Takeoff Ave.

          Josh

Go To ▶ Practice C on page 342.

- When you write a person's exact words, begin the first word with a capital letter.

  Examples: Mrs. Ling said, "**T**ell me about the museum."

  J. J. answered, "**I**t had some old airplanes."

- Begin the greeting and the closing of a postcard or a letter with a capital letter.

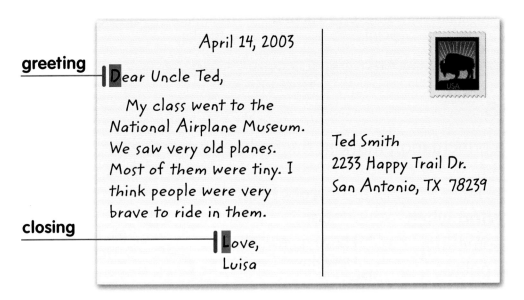

greeting ———

closing ———

April 14, 2003

Dear Uncle Ted,

My class went to the
National Airplane Museum.
We saw very old planes.
Most of them were tiny. I
think people were very
brave to ride in them.

Love,
Luisa

Ted Smith
2233 Happy Trail Dr.
San Antonio, TX 78239

- Each important word in a book title starts with a capital letter.

Shaka's **L**ong **T**rip

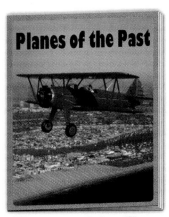

Planes of the **P**ast

Go To Practices D, E, and F on pages 342–343.

Grammar Made Graphic 287

Punctuation Marks

Punctuation marks make words and sentences easier to understand.

period | question mark | exclamation point | comma | quotation marks | apostrophe

End Marks

■ Always use a punctuation mark at the end of a sentence.

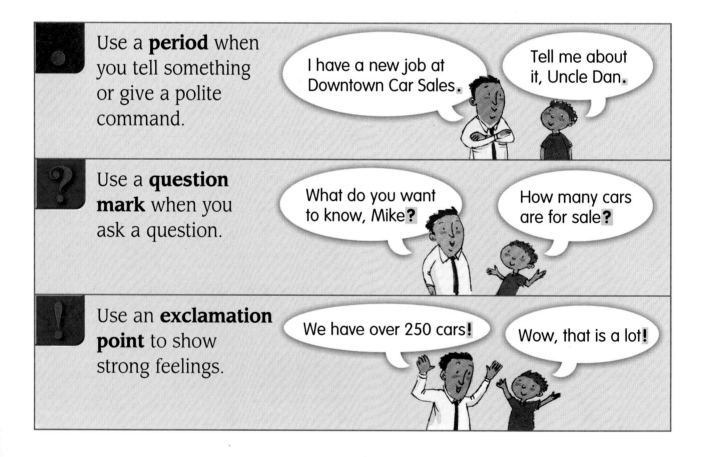

Use a **period** when you tell something or give a polite command.

> I have a new job at Downtown Car Sales.

> Tell me about it, Uncle Dan.

Use a **question mark** when you ask a question.

> What do you want to know, Mike?

> How many cars are for sale?

Use an **exclamation point** to show strong feelings.

> We have over 250 cars!

> Wow, that is a lot!

Go To Practice A on page 344.

More Ways to Use a Period

Use a **period** after the abbreviation of a place or of a person's title.

Mr. Blake works for Downtown Car Sales at 2456 N. Yale Ave. in Houston.

BUT: When you address an envelope or postcard to mail, you abbreviate the state name differently. Capitalize both letters and do **not** use a period.

Rick Foster
136 Motor Lane
Austin, **TX** 78759

Mark Berger
Downtown Car Sales
2456 N. Yale Ave.
Houston, **TX** 77074

TX is the abbreviation for Texas.

Use a **period** after an initial.

Mark R. Berger owns Downtown Car Sales.

Use a **period** when you write dollars and cents.

Sale
Save $900.00

Go To Practice B on page 344.

The Comma

Use **commas** when you write large numbers.

$58,000

Use **commas** when you write three or more items in a series.

Mr. Blake sells cars, vans, and trucks.

Sometimes he eats dinner, drives to work, and stays until 11 o'clock.

Use a **comma** after short words like **Oh**, **Yes**, and **Well** when they come at the beginning of a sentence.

Oh, you work at night.

Well, that is when many people buy cars.

You use **commas** a lot when you write a letter.

673 Hill Street
Chico, CA 95926
July 7, 2002

Dear Monika,
    Today I watched Uncle Dan sell cars. Mrs. Palmer picked out a red car. Then Uncle Dan took me to lunch. We had a great day!

        Your friend,
        Mike

Use a comma
- between the city and state
- between the day and the year
- after the greeting
- after the closing.

	Use a **comma** before **and**, **but**, or **or** in a compound sentence.	Mike visited Uncle Dan at work**, and** his uncle showed him all the cars. Mike watched Uncle Dan work**, but** he had to be quiet. Mike could go home for lunch**, or** he could go to a restaurant with his uncle.
	Use a **comma** before the exact words of a speaker.	Mike said**,** "Thanks for taking me to work." His uncle said**,** "You are welcome."

Go To ▶ Practices C and D on pages 344–345.

Quotation Marks

	Use **quotation marks** to show the exact words of a speaker.	Mrs. Palmer wanted to show her new car to her children. **"**I have a surprise for you,**"** Mrs. Palmer said. The children went outside. They saw the new car! **"**It is beautiful,**"** said Pam. Diane said, **"**I want to take a ride right now!**"**

Go To ▶ Practice E on page 345.

The Apostrophe

9 Use an **apostrophe** to show that a person or thing owns something.

Mom**'s** car
the girls**'** bikes
the car**'s** tires
the children**'s** dog

- Use **'s** to show that one person or thing owns something.

- Use **s'** to show that two or more people own something.

- Use **'s** when a plural noun does not end in **s**.

9 A **contraction** is a short form of two words. Every contraction has an **apostrophe**. It shows that one or more letters have been left out.

"**I'm** going to take you for a ride," said Mom. They **couldn't** wait to go! "**Don't** forget your seatbelts," she said.

After a while, Mom asked, "**Who's** ready for a snack? **Here's** an apple."

"**That's** a good snack," said Molly.

9

You can make a contraction from a verb
and the word **not**. Shorten **not** to **n't**.

is not = isn't	does not = doesn't
are not = aren't	did not = didn't
was not = wasn't	has not = hasn't
were not = weren't	have not = haven't
do not = don't	could not = couldn't

Spelling Tip

Some contractions
have special spellings.

will not = won't
can not = can't

You can make a contraction from a
pronoun or some other words and a verb.
Shorten the verb.

I am = I'm	who is = who's
you are = you're	here is = here's
he is = he's	you will = you'll
she is = she's	he will = he'll
it is = it's	she will = she'll
we are = we're	it will = it'll
they are = they're	we will = we'll
there is = there's	they will = they'll

Grammar Tip

Don't confuse **it's**
and **its**.

<u>it's</u> = it is
<u>its</u> is a pronoun

It's a very nice car.
Its stereo sounds really good!

Go To ▶ Practice F
on page 345.

Grammar Made Graphic

Chapter 6
Look It Up!

How do you turn questions into answers? Get the facts! Look things up in the library or on the Internet. Talk to people. Take notes. Share what you learn!

The Research Process

When you **research**, you look for information about something. You can use the information you find to give a talk, tell a story, or write a research report.

STEP 1 Choose a Topic

Think of something you want to learn about. This is your research **topic**.

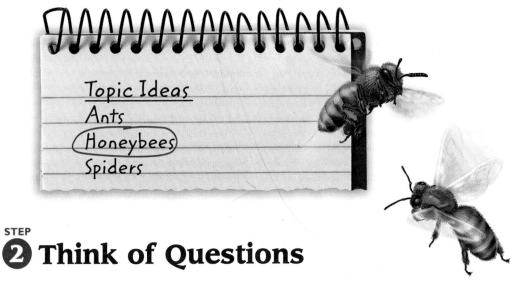

STEP 2 Think of Questions

Make a list of research questions about your topic.

Find the key words in your questions. Look up these words when you start your research.

③ Find Information

You can use different **resources** to find information about your topic.

books

encyclopedias

expert

An **expert** is someone who knows a lot about a topic.

Internet

magazines

You can start your research in a library. See pages 298–299 to find out more about a library.

Library

A library is a place that has many books, magazines, and other **resources**. It is organized in a special way to help you find things.

If you cannot find something, ask for help at the **Information Desk**.

One part of the library has **nonfiction** books. They have information about different topics.

The **Children's Room** has books for children.

The **card catalog** lists the books and other materials in the library. Most libraries have their card catalog on computer, too.

Reference Section

Information Desk

Nonfiction

Children's Room

The **Reference Section** has special books like dictionaries and encyclopedias.

Dictionary

Encyclopedia

The **Checkout Desk** is where you **check out**, or take home, books.

Magazines have articles in them. Most magazines are published every week or month.

You can use the library's **computers** to find information on the Internet.

Look It Up!

④ Take Notes

When you do research, write down important words and ideas. These **notes** help you remember the information.

■ First set up your notecards.

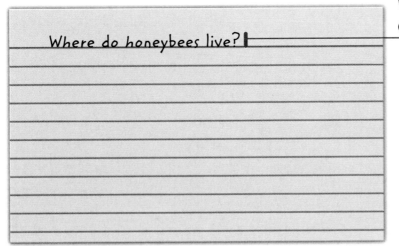

Where do honeybees live?

Write your **research question** at the top.

■ Find a good **source** of information.

THE HONEY MAKERS

GAIL GIBBONS

This book is an example of a **source**.

■ Find the page with the information you need.

■ Write the **source** on your notecard.

> Where do honeybees live?
>
> <u>The Honey Makers</u>, by Gail Gibbons, page 6

Write the **title** and underline it.

Write the **author**.

Write the **page number**.

Now you are ready to take notes.

④ Take Notes, continued

■ Write notes in **your own words**.

Book's words	Your own words

Book's words

Many honeybees like to make their homes in dark, enclosed places. Often a colony of wild honeybees builds its hive in a hollow tree.

Your own words

Many honeybees live in dark places like hollow trees.

Where do honeybees live?
The Honey Makers, by Gail Gibbons, p. 6
— Many honeybees live in

■ If you copy what you read, put **quotation marks** around the words.

Where do honeybees live?

The Honey Makers, by Gail Gibbons, page 6

— Many honeybees live in dark places like hollow trees.

— "Honeybees cared for by today's beekeepers live in box-shaped wooden hives."

■ Draw diagrams or other pictures that go with your notes.

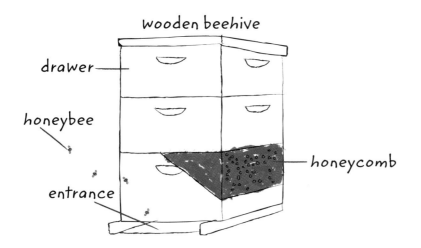

wooden beehive

drawer

honeybee

honeycomb

entrance

■ Think about the information, and ask new questions. Look for more answers.

What does the inside of a hive look like?

⑤ Make an Outline

Turn your notes into an **outline**. An outline is a plan for writing your report.

■ Look at your notecards. Group the cards for each research question.

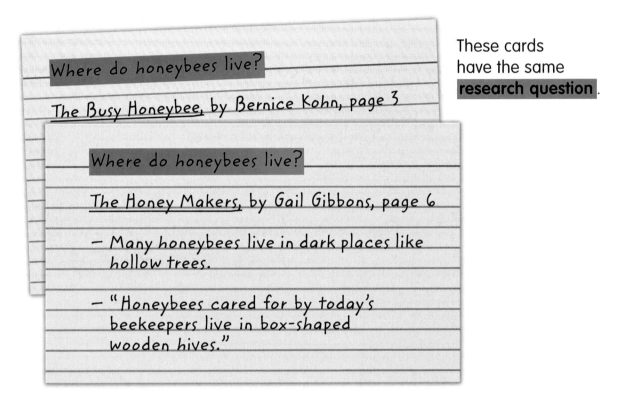

Where do honeybees live?

The Busy Honeybee, by Bernice Kohn, page 3

Where do honeybees live?

The Honey Makers, by Gail Gibbons, page 6

— Many honeybees live in dark places like hollow trees.

— "Honeybees cared for by today's beekeepers live in box-shaped wooden hives."

These cards have the same research question.

■ Turn your notes into an outline.

Turn each question into a **main idea**.

Then list **details** from your notes.

I. Where honeybees live
   A. Dark places like hollow trees
   B. Wooden boxes made by beekeepers

■ Here is an example of a finished outline.

Honeybees and Honey

A **Roman numeral** comes before each **main idea**.

I. Where honeybees live
  A. Dark places like hollow trees
  B. Wooden boxes made by beekeepers

A **capital letter** comes before each **detail**.

II. Inside the hives
  A. Sometimes more than 50,000 bees
  B. Mostly worker bees
  C. Honeycombs

III. How honeybees make honey
  A. Gather nectar from flowers
  B. Store nectar in cells
  C. Fan nectar with wings
  D. Nectar becomes honey

■ Think about what you learned. Write down any new questions. You can go back to answer those questions now or later.

Look It Up! 305

⑥ Turn Your Research into a Report

Now you are ready to write a **research report**.
Turn the main ideas and details from your outline
into sentences and paragraphs.

■ Look at the **title** of your outline. Can you
make it more interesting for your report?

Outline

Honeybees and Honey

**Title of
report**

Sweet Treats from Bees

■ Next, write an **introduction**. It is the first
paragraph of your report. The introduction
should be interesting. It should tell what
your report is mostly about.

Sweet Treats from Bees

Introduction   Can you imagine a house full of honey? You can
if you know about honeybees.

■ For the next paragraph, look at **Roman numeral I** on your outline. Turn this main idea into a **topic sentence**. Use the **important words** in a complete sentence.

Outline

Honeybees and Honey

I. Where honeybees live

Sweet Treats from Bees

Introduction   Can you imagine a house full of honey? You can if you know about honeybees.

Topic sentence   Honeybees live and make honey in different kinds of hives.

6 Turn Your Research into a Report, continued

■ Look at letters **A** and **B**. Turn these **details** into sentences that tell more about the main idea. Add them to your paragraph.

Outline

Honeybees and Honey

I. Where honeybees live
   A. Dark places like hollow trees
   B. Wooden boxes made by beekeepers

Sweet Treats from Bees

Introduction   Can you imagine a house full of honey? You can if you know about honeybees.

First paragraph   Honeybees live and make honey in different kinds of hives. A hive is a home for bees. Some honeybees build hives in hollow trees and in other dark places. Other honeybees live in wooden boxes made by beekeepers.

■ Write a paragraph for each Roman numeral on your outline.

■ Write a **conclusion**, or a summary of the most important information. The conclusion is the last paragraph. Look back at all the **main ideas** on your outline. Put them in your conclusion.

Outline

Honeybees and Honey

I. Where honeybees live
   A. Dark places like hollow trees
   B. Wooden boxes made by beekeepers

II. Inside the hives
   A. Sometimes more than 50,000 bees
   B. Mostly worker bees
   C. Honeycombs

III. How honeybees make honey
   A. Gather nectar from flowers
   B. Store nectar in cells
   C. Fan nectar with wings
   D. Nectar becomes honey

Conclusion

Honeybee hives are busy homes. Many honeybees work together to make and store honey inside their hives. Honeybees turn nectar from flowers into a sweet treat to eat.

7 Put It All Together!

Use pages 114–121 of **The Writing Process** to revise, proofread, and publish your research report. Include pictures, diagrams, graphs, or charts to explain information.

The **title** and **introduction** tell what your report is about. They get your reader interested.

The **body** of the report presents the facts you found.

Diagrams help your reader understand.

Sweet Treats from Bees

Can you imagine a house full of honey? You can if you know about honeybees.

Honeybees live and make honey in different kinds of hives. A hive is a home for bees. Some honeybees build hives in hollow trees and in other dark places. Other honeybees live in wooden boxes made by beekeepers.

It is crowded and busy inside a honeybee hive. A hive can have more than 50,000 honeybees. Most of them are worker bees. They build wax honeycombs that have thousands of small parts called cells. Worker bees store honey in most of the cells.

Honeycomb

— cell

— honey

It takes a lot of work to make honey! First, worker bees gather nectar from flowers. Nectar is a sweet liquid. The bees drink it. Then they return to the hive and spit up the nectar. Other worker bees store the nectar in cells. They fan the nectar with their wings to dry it out. The nectar gets thick and becomes honey for the bees to eat.

Honeybee hives are busy homes. Many honeybees work together to make and store honey inside their hives. Honeybees turn nectar from flowers into a sweet treat to eat.

Each paragraph in the body begins with a **topic sentence**. It tells a main idea. The other sentences give details.

The last paragraph is the **conclusion**. It sums up the report.

Research Tools

Books

Most nonfiction books have special parts at the front and back. These parts help you know what the book is about and how to find information in it.

Title Page

The **title page** is usually the first page in a book.

The title page gives the **full title** of the book.

The title page tells the **author**, or the person who wrote the book.

This is the **publisher**, or the company that made the book.

Honeybees at Work

by Shoko Yamada

Fun Books Company
San Antonio, Texas

Table of Contents

Some books have a **table of contents** after the title page. The table of contents lists the **chapters**, or main parts, of a book.

Table of Contents

The **chapter title** tells what the chapter is mostly about.

The **page number** tells what page the chapter begins on.

Glossary

A **glossary** is a short dictionary. It **defines**, or tells the meaning of, important words in a book. It appears near the end of the book.

The words are in alphabetical order by their first letter.

If words have the same first letter, look at the second letter.

Glossary

beekeeper — a person who raises bees for their honey

cell — a small, hollow place

colony — a large number of bees living together

hive — a structure where bees live

honey — a sweet, sticky liquid that bees make

honeybee — a bee that makes honey

honeycomb — a group of wax cells built by honeybees in their hive

34

Index

The **index** is at the back of a book. It tells where to find important ideas and words in the book.

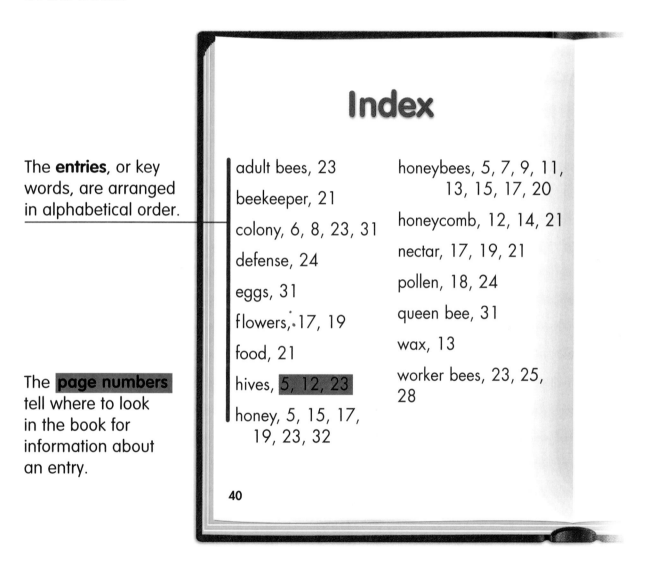

The **entries**, or key words, are arranged in alphabetical order.

The **page numbers** tell where to look in the book for information about an entry.

Index

40

Encyclopedia

An **encyclopedia** is a set of reference books with facts about many different topics. Each book is called a **volume**. The volumes are in alphabetical order.

How to Find Information in an Encyclopedia

1 What is the first letter of the word you want to look up? Find the volume for that letter. For example, if your topic is **rain forests**, look in the **R** volume.

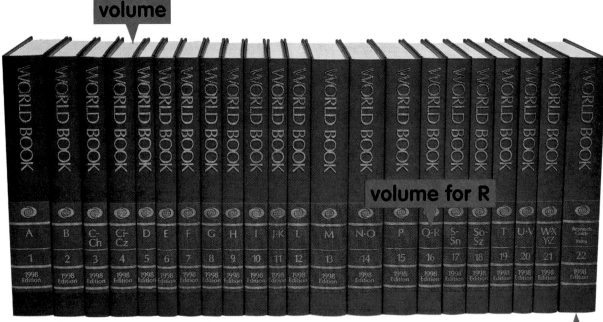

Most encyclopedias have a volume called an **index**. It lists other key words you can look up to find information about your topic.

2 Use alphabetical order to look up your word.

●Rain forest — **guide word**

Rain forest

article

Rain forests are thick forests of tall trees. They are found where the weather is warm the year around, and there is plenty of rain. Most rain forests grow near the equator, a make-believe line around Earth's middle. Africa, Asia, and Central and South America have large rain forests. Smaller rain forests are found in Australia and islands in the Pacific.

Tropical rain forests have more kinds of trees than anywhere else in the world. More than half of all the kinds of plants and animals on Earth live in tropical rain forests.

The tallest rain forest trees are as tall as 165 feet (50 meters). The treetops form a leafy covering called the canopy

Tropical rain forests have more kinds of trees than anywhere else in the world.

North America

Europe

Asia

Equator

Africa

South America

Australia

■ Rain forest area

Large rain forests are found in Africa, Asia, and Central and South America. Smaller rain forests are in Australia and islands in the Pacific.

180 The World Book Student Discovery Encyclopedia

Some encyclopedias are on a computer disk called a **CD-ROM**. You can read the information from the CD-ROM on your computer screen.

ENCYCLOPEDIA

Experts

An **expert** is someone who knows a lot about a topic. Ask questions, or **interview**, an expert to get answers about your topic.

Interviewing Tips

✔ Write down the questions you want to ask.

✔ Think of someone who might know a lot about your topic.

✔ Ask the person if he or she has time to answer your questions.

✔ Ask your questions clearly and politely.

✔ Listen carefully and take notes.

✔ Ask more questions if you do not understand something.

✔ Say thank you.

Magazines

Look for articles about your topic in magazines. Most magazines are published every week or month. Each magazine is called an **issue**.

The **magazine title** is on each issue.

The **date** tells when the issue was published.

These are some of the **topics** in the issue.

This is the **main topic** in the issue.

National Wildlife Federation

Ranger Rick

January 2002

No-Snow Penguins

Where Do Insects Go in Winter?

All About Snakes

COYOTES Good Neighbors or Bad?

Internet

The **Internet** is a connection of computers that share information through the **World Wide Web**. You can find information on the Internet.

How to Do Research on the Web

1 Click twice on an **icon** to get into the Internet. An icon is a picture on your computer screen.

2 Go to a **search page**. Type your key words in the search box. Then click on **Search**.

This is a **toolbar**. Click on the pictures to do what they say.

Type your key words here.

Click here to **search**, or look for, your key words.

Look It Up!

3 Read the list of **Web sites**, or pages, that have your key words. The underlined words are **links** to the Web sites.

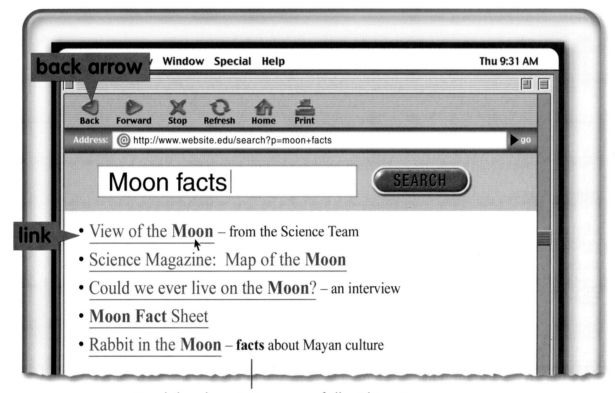

Read the descriptions carefully. This site may be interesting, but it may not help you with your report.

4 Click on a link to go directly to the **site**, or **Web page**. If you want to go back to the list of Web sites, click on the **back arrow**.

Sentences

A. Finish each sentence. Use an ending from the box.
Write the sentence.

all weekend.	come to the city?	can see a movie.
say it's okay!	Friday night!	I come?
your parents.	movies!	to get there!

question **1.** Can you _____

statement **2.** We _____

exclamation **3.** Wow, I love _____

question **4.** When can _____

command **5.** Come on _____

statement **6.** I can stay _____

command **7.** First, ask _____

exclamation **8.** They _____

exclamation **9.** I can't wait _____

B. Add *not* or *never* to make a negative
sentence. Write the sentence.

1. Tomás walks to school. He _____ rides the bus.

2. He is _____ here this morning.

3. He was _____ at school yesterday.

4. He _____ misses school. I hope he is okay.

C. Add a subject. Write the sentence.

1.

plays with his dog in the park.

subject   predicate

2.

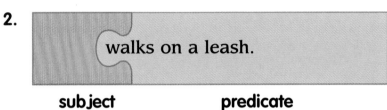

walks on a leash.

subject   predicate

3.

are in the park, too.

subject   predicate

D. Add a predicate. Write the sentence.

1.

Mom

subject   predicate

2.

The children

subject   predicate

3.

The brown dog

subject   predicate

E. Write each compound sentence.
   Use the correct word.

1. Anna visits Granny, ___and / but___ they go to the street fair.

2. They want to take a cab, ___or / but___ it costs too much.

3. "We can take a bus, ___or / and___ we can walk,"
   says Granny.

4. "I like to walk, ___and / but___ it is too far," says Anna.

5. Soon a bus comes, ___and / or___ they get on.

6. "Do you want to sit here, ___but / or___ do you like
   the window seat?" Granny asks.

F. Join the sentences. Use a word from the box.
   Write the new sentence.

| and | but | or |

1. At the fair, Granny plays games. Anna goes on
   rides.

2. Granny has plain popcorn. Anna asks for
   popcorn with butter.

3. The next day they can come back to the fair. They can
   go to the movies.

Nouns

A. Write these sentences. Add the correct nouns.

| lake | Anna | people | ducks | Park Street |

1. ____ takes a walk with her father.

2. They walk to ____ .

3. They see many ____ in the stores.

4. Then they walk by a ____ in the park.

5. Anna watches the ____ in the water.

B. Copy the chart. Write the plural of each noun in the second column. Then draw a picture to go with each noun.

	One	More than One
1.	book	
2.	bowl	
3.	dish	
4.	cake	
5.	penny	
6.	foot	
7.	berry	
8.	child	

C. Choose the correct word to complete each sentence. Write the sentence.

1. Efram's family wants to hear ___a / an___ concert.

2. They see ___a / an___ ad for a concert.

3. They decide to go to ___an / the___ concert that night.

4. The family rides ___a / an___ bus that goes to the city.

5. It takes almost ___a / an___ hour to get there!

6. Efram wants to sit close to ___an / the___ stage.

7. ___The / A___ music sounds great!

D. Write these sentences. Use the correct possessive noun.

1. Kay has a bike. ___Kay's / Kays'___ bike is brand new.

2. Kay has two brothers. Her ___brother's / brothers'___ bikes are not new.

3. One ___boy's / boys___ bike has a flat tire.

4. Mr. Bill will fix the ___bikes' / bike's___ tire.

E. Write the paragraph. Replace the underlined words with precise nouns. Tell about your city or town.

Let's take a walk down <u>the street</u>. We will smell delicious <u>food</u> at the restaurant. Maybe <u>people</u> will play <u>music</u> on the sidewalk. We will see many beautiful <u>things</u> in the windows of <u>the store</u>. We will have fun in <u>this town</u>.

Pronouns

**A. Write these sentences.
Use the correct pronoun.**

1. Aunt Sue comes to the city.

"_**They / She**_ visits Clare and Ray.

2. Clare shows Aunt Sue a bedroom.

"_**It / You**_ can sleep here," Clare says.

3. Ray and Clare show Aunt Sue the city.

**They / He** all take a walk.

4. Aunt Sue takes the children into the library.

"_**We / I**_ will each get a book," Aunt Sue says.

5. Ray checks out a book to read.

**You / He** also checks out one for Aunt Sue.

6. Clare points outside.

"_**I / He**_ see a man selling pretzels," Clare says.

7. Aunt Sue buys some pretzels.

**They / It** are warm and salty.

8. Ray points to a bench.

"_**He / We**_ can sit and eat," Ray says.

Grammar Practice

B. Write these sentences. Use the correct pronoun.

1. Clare and Ray paint pictures of ___their / they___ town.

2. Clare draws ___she / her___ house.

3. She shows ___its / it___ front yard.

4. She does not have red paint for the flowers. "May I use ___you / your___ red paint?" she asks Ray.

5. Ray draws ___her / his___ school.

6. "Here is ___I / my___ teacher," Ray says.

7. "We can send the pictures to ___we / our___ grandparents," Clare says.

8. Grandma and Grandpa like the pictures. They put the pictures on ___their / its___ wall.

C. Write these sentences. Use the correct pronoun.

1. We clean up our neighborhood. There is a job for each of ___us / our___.

2. Clare and Ray are there. The leader asks ___they / them___ to rake the leaves.

3. Dad wants a job, too. "What do you want ___me / I___ to do?" he asks.

4. We tell ___he / him___ to put the leaves in a bag.

5. Dad fills the bag and carries ___it / them___ to the truck.

Subject Pronouns	Object Pronouns
I	me
you	you
he, she, it	him, her, it
we	us
they	them

D. Write these sentences. Use the correct word.

1. _This / These_ park needs to be cleaned up.

2. _That / Those_ girls will plant flowers.

3. I will paint _that / this_ bench over there.

4. Put the trash in _these / this_ bags.

5. _These / This_ neighborhood has a great park!

E. Write the paragraph. Replace the underlined words with the correct pronoun.

The neighbors on our block want to have a party. The neighbors want to have the party this weekend! Mrs. Brown is knocking on all the doors. Mrs. Brown is asking people to prepare a dish. Everyone likes Mrs. Brown, so they all say "yes." The party is going to be a great party!

Adjectives

A. Write these sentences. Add an adjective. Choose one from the box or think of one yourself.

clean	tall
bright	shiny
long	red
low	big
high	white

1. The train passed through the ____ mountains.

2. All the cars were ____ .

3. The train looked like a ____ snake.

4. It went over a ____ bridge.

5. At night, you could see the train's ____ light.

B. Write these sentences. Add an adjective from the box.

| thirty |
| much |
| One |
| Some |
| many |

1. There are so ____ cars in this train!

2. It has about ____ cars.

3. ____ trains have more cars.

4. ____ engine drives the train.

5. It does not take ____ time to get to the city.

C. Write these sentences. Use the correct adjective to make a comparison.

1. Bicycles are ____slower / slowest____ than cars.

2. Of all the ways to travel, rockets are the ____faster / fastest____ .

3. Trucks can carry ____heavier / heaviest____ loads than cars.

4. Trucks are ____noisier / noisiest____ than cars.

5. Bikes are the ____quieter / quietest____ of all.

6. Big cities have the ____busier / busiest____ streets of any place.

7. For the ____cleaner / cleanest____ bike, scrub with soap and water.

8. I think blue is a ____prettier / prettiest____ color for a car than black.

D. Write these sentences. Use the correct adjective to make a comparison.

1. This road goes through the beautifulest / most beautiful
   part of town.

2. My most favorite / most favoritest part is the bridge.

3. You can see the best / goodest view from there.

4. The road is bumpy, but it is more good / better
   than Ford Road.

5. Traffic is worse / more worse there.

6. Ford Road is also more dangerous / dangerouser
   because it is curvy.

7. The baddest / worst time to drive is when
   the road is wet.

8. The more important / most important thing
   of all is to go slowly.

E. Write a description of a car or a bicycle you like. Use adjectives to help your readers picture it clearly.

Verbs

A. Write each sentence. Add a verb from the box.

1. We ____ at the playground.

2. The sun ____ hot.

3. I ____ on the swings.

4. My sister ____ at the pond.

5. My friends ____ on the slide.

6. Elena ____ at the top.

7. Mark ____ on the ladder.

8. They ____ happy!

am
are
is

B. Write each sentence. Use the correct verb.

1. We ___have / has___ soccer practice on Saturday morning.

2. The coach ___have / has___ two helpers.

3. Each helper ___have / has___ a group of kids.

4. The kids ___have / has___ one hour to practice.

5. Then we ___have / has___ one hour to play a game.

6. When we get home, Mom ___have / has___ lunch ready.

7. We ___have / has___ so much fun on Saturday morning!

Grammar Practice

C. Write each sentence. Use the correct verb.

1. I ___play / plays___ baseball every day.

2. I ___pitch / pitches___ the ball to Sam.

3. He ___hit / hits___ the ball.

4. Then he ___runs / run___ to a base.

5. Lisa ___catch / catches___ the ball.

6. She ___throw / throws___ the ball to me.

7. Sam ___tries / try___ to run to the next base.

8. I ___tag / tags___ him. Sam is out.

9. We ___wins / win___ the game.

10. We ___cheer / cheers___ for our team.

D. Write each sentence. Add the correct form of the red verb.

play **1.** We ____ soccer after school.

shout **2.** The coach ____ to the players.

watch **3.** My dad ____ the game.

hurry **4.** Berto ____ after the ball.

kick **5.** He ____ the ball to me.

score **6.** I ____ a goal.

wave **7.** My dad ____ to me.

bark **8.** My dog ____.

clap **9.** My friends ____.

jump **10.** We ____ up and down.

E. Make a chart. Write each underlined verb in the correct column.

Now	In the Past

1. Pablo and I <u>like</u> soccer.

2. Yesterday we <u>biked</u> to the park.

3. We <u>played</u> a good game of soccer.

4. Today Pablo <u>calls</u> me on the phone.

5. I <u>hurry</u> over to Pablo's house.

6. We <u>watch</u> a good game of soccer on T.V.

F. Write each sentence. Add -ed to change the underlined verb to the past tense.

1. I <u>walk</u> to baseball practice.

2. I <u>chase</u> each ball.

3. I <u>rush</u> around the field.

4. I <u>jump</u> up to make a catch.

5. After practice, I <u>rest</u>!

G. Write each sentence. Change the underlined verb to the past tense. Use the chart to help you.

1. I <u>go</u> to the pool every day.

2. I <u>bring</u> my friend Mai.

3. Mai <u>knows</u> how to swim.

4. We <u>take</u> our lunch to the pool.

5. First, Mai <u>dives</u> into the pool.

6. Then, she <u>holds</u> her breath from one end of the pool to the other.

7. Next, Mai <u>does</u> the backstroke.

8. We <u>keep</u> busy all day.

9. The lifeguard <u>sees</u> us in the water.

10. He <u>says</u>, "Good work!"

Now	In the Past
bring	brought
dive	dove
do	did
go	went
keep	kept
know	knew
say	said
see	saw
take	took
hold	held

Grammar Practice

H. Write each sentence. Use the correct verb.

1. I ___was / were___ at the pool all day yesterday.

2. My friend and I ___was / were___ there to practice for the race.

3. I ___was / were___ glad to have my friend with me.

4. Other people from school ___was / were___ there, too.

5. But they ___was / were___ not there all day, like us!

6. The water ___was / were___ cold at first, but we got used to it.

7. When we left, we ___was / were___ really tired.

8. Our fingers ___was / were___ all wrinkled from the water.

I. Write each sentence. Use the correct verb.

1. Every night I ___listen / listened___ to the news, and I find out about the weather.

2. Yesterday it ___snow / snowed___ a lot.

3. All the kids ___stay / stayed___ home from school.

4. Tomorrow the sun ___shined / is going to shine___.

5. The sun ___melted / will melt___ the snow.

6. When the snow is gone, we ___will play / played___ in the park.

J. Write each statement or question. Use the correct verb.

1. We ___is / are___ going to the park today.

2. ___Do / Does___ you want to play?

3. You ___is / can___ be on my team.

4. ___Is / Are___ Tina throwing the ball to Felipe?

5. Yes. He ___might / am___ catch it.

6. ___Is / Are___ he jumping up to get it?

7. I ___are / am___ reaching for it, too.

8. My friends ___are / is___ shouting at me!

9. I ___does / do___ not drop it. I catch it!

10. ___Does / Do___ my team cheer? Yes, they do!

K. Write two or three sentences about a sport or an outdoor activity that you like. Use colorful verbs.

Adverbs

**A. Write these sentences. Add an adverb.
Choose one from the box or think of one yourself.**

1. Josh and Aunt Sue went to the
science museum _____.

2. They saw dinosaurs _____.

3. The dinosaurs roared _____!

4. Josh _____ realized that the dinosaurs
were just robots.

loudly
there
quickly
today

5. Josh and Aunt Sue wandered _____.

6. They studied every exhibit _____.

7. Aunt Sue _____ said it was time to go.

8. Josh _____ loves to visit the science museum!

around
finally
always
carefully

**B. Write a paragraph about a visit to a museum,
a circus, or some other interesting place.
Use adverbs to tell when, where, and how.**

Capital Letters

A. Write each sentence. Use capital letters correctly.

1. a pilot came to mrs. Smith's class.

2. his name was Captain charles worth.

3. the children had many questions for Captain Worth.

4. Betty jasper and i asked how long it took to learn to fly.

5. some kids wanted to know if it is hard to fly.

B. Write each sentence. Use capital letters correctly.

1. Betty's family took an airplane trip in may.

2. They flew on memorial day.

3. The holiday was on a monday.

4. They will go again on labor day.

5. That will be in september.

6. They will be there on saturday, sunday, and monday.

C. Write each sentence. Use capital letters correctly.

1. The class visited Captain Worth at central airport.

2. The airport is on elm st. in boulder city.

3. The pilot flies in canada and in the united states.

4. "This afternoon, I will fly from california to ohio," he said.

5. "I love to see the pacific ocean from the air," the pilot said.

D. Write this letter. Use capital letters correctly.

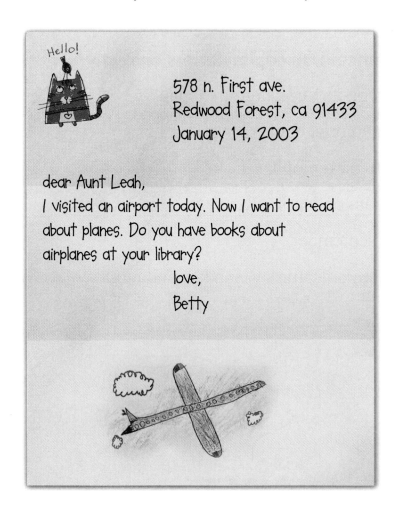

Hello!

578 n. First ave.
Redwood Forest, ca 91433
January 14, 2003

dear Aunt Leah,
I visited an airport today. Now I want to read
about planes. Do you have books about
airplanes at your library?
love,
Betty

E. Write this list of book titles. Use capital letters correctly.

1. *first book of airplanes*

2. *become a pilot*

3. *taro takes a ride*

4. *airplanes, helicopters, and balloons*

5. *history of travel*

6. *mystery at midtown airport*

F. Write each sentence. Use capital letters correctly.

1. betty took a trip with john, her uncle, to shell beach.

2. they rented a boat and went to turtle island.

3. ms. king gave them a book called *boat safety*.

4. they paddled around oak bay.

5. john said, "it is hot for early june."

6. betty said, "we can stop at the island and sit under a tree."

Punctuation

A. Write each sentence. Add the correct punctuation at the end.

1. What job does your mother do

2. She drives a truck for a flower shop

3. Please take these flowers to the hospital

4. Wow, what a great job I have

B. Write each sentence. Add periods where they belong.

1. Mom's boss is J W Daffodil.

2. Mr Daffodil is a very nice man.

3. He charges $27 50 for a bunch of roses.

C. Write the following letter. Add commas where they are needed.

Flores Flower Shop
10 Major Lane
Chester Maryland   21009
August 5 2003

Dear Mrs. Flores
You take good care of the flowers. You drive
safely. Thank you for doing a great job.

Sincerely

Marcos

D. Write each sentence. Add commas where they are needed.

1. Mr. Waters used to own a restaurant but now he owns a gas station.

2. Mr. Waters sells gas oil snacks and soft drinks.

3. Well he also sells newspapers and maps.

4. The station opens at 8:00 in the morning and Mr. Waters spends all day there.

E. Write the following sentences. Add commas and quotation marks where they are needed.

1. I want to buy a truck said Dad.

2. Mike answered A truck is useful!

3. Yes, I can carry things said Dad.

4. Dad told Mike You can pick the color of the truck.

5. Mike said OK. I like red for a truck.

F. Write the following sentences. Add apostrophes where they are needed.

1. Dads new truck is parked in the alley.

2. Hes going to take our bikes to the beach in his truck.

3. Dad doesnt want to hurt the new truck.

4. Dad is careful when he opens the trucks door.

5. He hopes the truck wont get scratched or dented.

Index

A

A, an, and the, 248–249, 326
Abbreviations, 289
Actions, 18
    See also Verbs
Address, 16, 132, 133, 136, 289, 290, 342, 344
Adjectives
    in writing, 267, 332
    kinds, 262–263, 330–331
    placement in a sentence, 266
    that compare, 264–265, 331–332
    See also Antonyms; Describing words;
       Multiple-meaning words; Synonyms
Adverbs, 282–283, 340
Advertisements, 139
Alphabet
    cursive, 199
    manuscript, 195
Alphabetical order, 230, 314
And, but, and or, 239–240, 324
Announcement, 122
Antonyms, 74–75, 170, 171
Apostrophe
    in contractions, 292–293, 345
    with possessive nouns, 250, 292, 345
Article (of an encyclopedia), 317
Articles
    See **A, an,** and **the**
Audience, 109, 166–167, 182–189, 194
Author, 123, 301, 312

B

Body parts, 61
Book review, 123
Book parts, 312–315
    glossary, 314
    index, 315
    table of contents, 313
    title page, 312

C

Capital letters
    beginning of a sentence, 172, 197, 234, 284,
    341–343
    days and months, 285, 341
    in abbreviations, 285–286, 342
    in an outline, 305
    in dialogue, 287, 343
    in greetings and closings, 287, 342
    pronoun *I*, 284, 341
    proper nouns, 284–287, 341–343

Captions, 131
Card catalog, 298
CD-ROM, 317
Character, 98, 129, 150
    See also Clusters; Story maps
Charts
    definition, 86
    FATP chart, 109
    5Ws chart, 110
    KWL chart, 87
Classroom objects, 40–41
Clothes, 70–71
Clusters
    character map, 89
    for prewriting, 110
    web, 88, 159
Colors, 20, 21
Comma
    in a compound sentence, 240, 291, 345
    in a series, 290
    in dialogue, 291, 345
    in letters, 290, 344
    to set off certain words, 290
    with large numbers, 290
Community, 56–59
Community workers, 58–59
Comparisons, 142, 264–265
Compound sentences, 240, 324
Compound subjects and predicates
    See **And, but,** and **or**
Compound words, 76–77
Computers
    CD-ROM, 317
    drafting, 113
    e-mail, 128
    in a library, 299
    Internet, 297, 299, 320–321
    publishing, 121
    saving ideas, 159
    spell check, 118–119
Conclusion, 309, 311
Conjunctions
    See **And, but,** and **or**
Contractions, 292–293, 345
    spelling *it's, they're, you're*, 224–225
Conversation
    See Discussion

D

Days of the week, 66, 285
Demonstrative pronouns
    See **This, that, these,** and **those**

S

T

Acknowledgments, continued

Batista Moon Studio: p297 and p316 (encyclopedias).

Bruce Coleman, Inc.: p71 (fall, © Barbara Williams), p136 (alligator, © John Shaw).

Cartesia: p3, p10 and p180 (map).

Corbis: (all © Corbis) p23 (noisy, © James L. Amos), p25 (smooth skin, © Barbara P. Williams), p25 (wet hair, © DigitalStock), p28 (house, © Lester Leftkowitz/Corbis Stock Market), p58 (farmer, © Ed Bock/Corbis Stock Market), p70 (summer, © Michael Keller/Corbis Stock Market), p75 (fast, © DigitalStock), p77 (rainbow, © DigitalStock; waterfall, ©Kevin R. Morris), p81 (train, © Alan Carey; jam, © DigitalStock), p82 (blue, © DigitalStock), p136 (Everglades, © David Muench), p141 (making salsa), p155 (Tokyo, © B.S.P.I.), p176 (soccer, © Tim Pannell/Corbis Stock Market), p193 (dog, © DigitalStock), p203 (Earth from

moon, © DigitalStock), p205 and p211 (fish, © DigitalStock), p208 (kiss, © DigitalStock), p210 (Ox, © Jack Fields), p211 (whale, © DigitalStock), p213 (frog and sky, © DigitalStock), p214 (sea, © DigitalStock; feet, © Jerry Tobias), p215 (boat, © DigitalStock), p216 (city, © DigitalStock), p217 (bird, © DigitalStock), p218 (moon, © DigitalStock), p297 and p299 (flowers, © DigitalStock).

Digital Studios: p41 (glue), p75 (empty and full), p76 (bathtub, flashlight, and backpack), p87 (notebook), p98, p150 and pp152-153 (book), p195 and p199 (pencil), p190 and p191 (computer), p205 and p210 (egg), p211 (bath), p213 (stamp), p246 (glass and dish), p299 (dictionary).

John Paul Endress: p206 (back), p209 (six and zero), p211 (match), p212 (old belt), p214 (cake and tie), p215 (fruit and tube), p216 (cot).

FoodPix: p74 (hot chocolate, ©Evan Sklar).

Getty Images, Inc.: (all © Getty Images, Inc.) p4 and p15 (open book, © Siede Preis/PhotoDisc), p31 (bathroom © Rob Melnychuk/PhotoDisc), p41 (pencil, pen, chalk, ruler, scissors, eraser, and crayon, © Artville), p45 (one dollar, five dollars, ten dollars, twenty dollars, penny, nickel, dime, and quarter, © Artville), p59 (judge, © Jeff Cadge/The Image Bank), p70 (rain, © Darrell Gulin/The Image Bank), p74 and p171 (elephant and mouse, © PhotoDisc), p74 (glass, © John A. Rizzo/PhotoDisc), p75 (day, © PhotoDisc; night, © Adrian Pope/Taxi; new, © Artville; old, © Christian Michaels/Taxi), p76 (baseball, © Artville; sailboat and mailbox, © PhotoDisc), p77 (popcorn, © Artville; sailboat and mailbox, © PhotoDisc), p80 (bark, baseball bat, and bat, © PhotoDisc; bank, © Ryan McVay/PhotoDisc; riverbank, © Michael Busselle/Stone), p81 (leaves, © Michael Melford/The Image Bank), p82 (eight, © PhotoDisc; blew, © Terry Qing/Taxi), p83 (sail, © PhotoDisc; won, © Mike

Powell/Allsport Concepts), p142 (father and son, © Art Wolfe/The Image Bank), p154 (girl typing, © John Terence Turner/Taxi), p155 (Tokyo, © V.C.L./Taxi), p156 (corn and popcorn, © Artville; mother and daughter picking corn, © Paul Chesley/Stone), p159, p297, p299, and p317 (computer, © Duncan Smith/PhotoDisc), p167 (swimming lesson, © Tracy Frankel/The Image Bank), p204 (ball, © Artville; cat, © PhotoDisc), p205 (leaf, cuff, pig and hand © PhotoDisc; jar, © Artville), p206 (key, beak, heel, and map, © PhotoDisc; bell, © EyeWire Collection; lamp, © Janis Christie/PhotoDisc; drum, © Artville), p207 (net, knife, and pizza, © C Squared Studios/PhotoDisc; can, © Artville; cup, sign, and quilt, © PhotoDisc), p208 (wrist, seed, hat, and ten, © PhotoDisc; van and mitt, © Artville), p210 (apple and pin, © PhotoDisc; man, © EyeWire Collection; inch, © Artville), p211 (shell and thumb, © PhotoDisc; peach, © Artville; ring, © C Squared Studios/PhotoDisc), p212 (gift, hand, bank, and disk, © PhotoDisc; lamp, © Janis Christie/PhotoDisc; ant, © Paul Beard/PhotoDisc; nest, © Ryan McVay/PhotoDisc), p213 (truck, © Donovan Reese/PhotoDisc; flag, © PhotoDisc; drum, © Artville), p214 (sail and night, © PhotoDisc; bunny, © G.K. & Vikki Hart/PhotoDisc), p215 (rope, © Spike Mafford/PhotoDisc; toe, © Jack Hollingsworth/PhotoDisc), p216 (cup and cat, © PhotoDisc; rice, © Ryan McVay/PhotoDisc; gem, © Lawrence Lawry/PhotoDisc; cent and ginger, © Artville), p217 (horn, © C Squared Studios/PhotoDisc; chair, © Ryan McVay/PhotoDisc; tear, © Paul Dance/Stone; deer, © Jules Frazier/PhotoDisc; fern, © PhotoDisc), p218 (cent, © Artville; cloud and boy, © PhotoDisc; crown, © C Squared Studios/PhotoDisc), p219 (ball, © Artville; saw, © PhotoDisc), p222 (babies, puppy, and puppies, © PhotoDisc; glasses, © Artville), p246 (cat, © PhotoDisc; lunch, ©Artville), p281 (ice skater, © Lori Adamski Peek/Stone), p287 (train, © Digital Vision), p297 (expert, © David Barnes/Stone) p297 and p299 (bee, © Artville).

Image Club Graphics, Inc.: p204 (cab), p213 (clock), p217 (star), p218 (screw), p219 (salt), p222 (box).

Index Stock Imagery, Inc.: pp54-55 (city park, © James Blank), p59 (fireman, © Doug Mazell), p80 (bark, © Barry Winiker), p125 (garden, © Gay Bumgarner), p181 (kids in El Salvador, © Alyx Kellington), p283 (dinosaur, © Stewart Cohen), p287 (biplane, © Larry McManus).

Lonely Planet Images: p181 (El Salvador mountain, © Kraig Lieb; El Salvador statue, people, and fishing boats, © Charlotte Hindle).

Lunar Planetary Institute: p321 (moon).

MetaPhotos: p209 (wagon).

NASA: p191 (shuttle).

New Century Graphics: p3, p13, and p295 (book), p3, p13, and p295 (magnifying glass),

p9, p107, and p121 (printer), p46 (buttons), p68 (clocks), p74 (shoe and box), p75 (clean and dirty), p96 (pens), p113 (computer), p126 (maracas , bottles, and beads), p130 (journal and crayon), p133 (stamp), p135 (Mancala), p136 and p287 (stamp), p158 (rainbow card), p158 (notebook), p159 (index cards and box, notebook), p169 (duffel bag), p172 (clock), p178 (Review Your Writing), p216 (gum).

Peter Arnold, Inc.: p213 and p215 (crow).

PhotoEdit, Inc.: p29 (townhouse, © David Young-Wolff), p39 (principal, © Michael Newman), p58 (dentist, © Bill Aron; cashier, © David Young-Wolff), p59 (waiter and police officer, © Rhoda Sidney), p81 (train, © Jeff Greenberg; kids taking turns, © David Young-Wolff), p83 (sale, © Robert Brenner), p124 (boys, © Myrleen Ferguson Cate), p144 (kids in line, © David Young-Wolff).

PictureQuest LLC: (all © PictureQuest LLC) p29 (mobile home, © Michael Dwyer/Stock Boston, Inc.), p132 (Chinese Dragon, © Allen Russell/Index Stock Imagery), p217 (bear, © Fransisco Erize/Bruce Coleman, Inc.), p221 (kids skipping, © IT Int'l/eStock Photography).

Stockbyte: p77, p213, and p222 (hairbrush), p77 (keyboard), p83 (father and son), p137 (ingredients), p171 (baby), p210 and p222 (pot), p213 (plant), p219 (launch), p246 (flower).

StockFood: p209 (fizz, © Eising Food Photography).

SuperStock, Inc.: p71 (winter), p83 (sun, © Larry Chiger).

Elizabeth Garza Williams: p3, p10-11, and pp180-181 (speech), p5 (hello), p6 (boy writing), p8 (girl with notecard), p12 (kids), p14 (girl), pp14-15, p16, p72, pp84-85, pp106-107, p180, p232, and p294 (chalkboard), pp16-17 (Words About You), p18 (Actions), p19 (Feelings), p20 (Colors), p21 (Shapes), p22 (Sizes), p23 (whispering, girl plugging ears, and boy with trumpet), p24 (Smells), p25 (Touch), pp26-27 (Taste), p28 (girl), p29 (apartment), p30 (girl, kitchen, living room, and bedroom), p32 (boy), p33 (family and relatives), pp34-35 (Words About Your School), pp36-37 (Inside the School), p38 (teacher and students), p39 (librarian, nurse, custodian, and boy), p40 (In a Classroom), pp41-43 (Things to Do), p44 (counting buttons), p46 (girl with buttons), p47 (Number Order), p48 (Say Hello), p49 (Say Good-bye), p50 (Say Thank You), p51 (Meet New People), pp52-53 (Ask for Help), p54 (girl), p56 (kids), p58 (boy), pp60-61 (Doctor's Office), p62 (girl), pp64-65 (Signs and Safety), p69 (Telling Time), p70 (summer girl, spring boy, fall boy, and winter girl), p74 (up, down, stop, go, good, and bad), p75 (happy and sad), p76 (classroom and fingernail), p77 (sidewalk), p78 (Suffixes), p79 (Prefixes), p81 (jam, leave, and turn), p82 (hole, whole, and ate), p83 (one, write, and right), p84 (boy), p104 (boy), p106 (boy), p108, p109, and p111 (The Writing Process),

p114 (piñata), p115 (Revise), p116 (girl eating), p130 (boy writing), p132 (girl writing), p133 (girl mailing), p134 (girl reading), p138 and 139 (kids gardening), p146 (Rainy Day), p170 (boy reading), p172 (kids talking), p175 (girl with bag), p179 (Think About Your Writing), p182 (Read Aloud), p183 (Listen to a Story), p184 (Give a Message), p185 (Get a Message), p188 (Talk in a Group), p189 (Listen in a Group), p190 (cutting pictures out, looking at dictionary), p191 (boy with chart), p194 (Handwriting and Spelling Guide), p204 (desk), p205 and p216 (gate), p210 (bus and up), p211 (chin), p213 (smell), p214, p222 and p246 (kite), p216 (go), p217 (turn), p221 (girl reading), p223 (girl), p232 (Grammar Made Graphic), p246 (box), p288 (girl reading), p294 and p302 (boy typing), p297 (library), p301 (boy with pencil), p307 and p311 (girl typing), p318 (Experts).

Illustrations:

All illustrations by Lynne Cravath unless otherwise noted.

All children's illustrations by Damon Swisher.

Cover illustration by Stephen Durke.

Rick Allen: pp152-153 (The Rabbit, The Coyote and the Big Rock); **Doug Bekke:** p198 (alligator); **Annie Bissett:** p90 (Oak Tree), p91 (Life of an Oak Tree), p97 (U.S. Map); **Peter Grosshauser:** p7 (The Fox and the Crow), pp56-57 (In Your Community), p57 (Words That Tell Where), pp62-63 (Transportation), p67 (Seasons), p98 (Anansi and Turtle), p100 (fox and The Fox and the Crow), p147 (Tommy background), p193 (pet store and library); **Robert Hynes:** p150 (Story and The Little Lost Whale); **Loretta Lustig:** p129 (The Ant and the Bird); **Paul Mirocha:** p190 (map), p296 (honey bees), p313 (bee); **Francisco Mora:** p102 (The Fox in the Moon); **Ilene Richard:** pp72-73 (Synonyms), p148 (Limerick), pp224-225 (Spell These Right!); **Roni Shepherd:** p99 (The Ants and the Grasshopper and flower border), p149 (Ears Hear), p220 (dinosaur eating and under palm tree); **Robbie Short:** pp298-299 (library); **Krystyna Stasiak:** p89 (Little Red Riding Hood); **Lane Yerkes:** p101 (It Could Always Be Worse).

***English At Your Command!*
Development Team**

Editorial: Julie Cason, Roseann Erwin, Dawn Liseth, Sheron Long, Jacalyn Mahler, Stephen Newitt, C. M. Antoinette Nichols, Juan Quintana, Andrea Weiss, and Ink, Inc.

Design and Production: Mary Helen Aguirre-Greenwood, Sherry Corley, Jeri Gibson, Raymond Ortiz Godfrey, Raymond Hoffmeyer, Stephanie Rice, Augustine Rivera, Susan Scheuer, Curtis Spitler, Jonni Stains, Alicia Sternberg, Terry Taylor, Teri Wilson.

Permissions: Barbara Mathewson.